MACHINE

LEARNING

WITH

PYTHON

2 books in 1

PYTHON FOR BEGINNERS

PYTHON for DATA SCIENCE

JASON TEST MARK BROKER

Learn the art of programming with a complete

crash course for beginners.

Strategies to master data science, numpy, keras,

pandas and arduino like a pro in 7 days

CONTENTS

MACHINE LEARNING with PYTHON

PYTHON FOR BEGINNERS

Python code optimization with ctypes 26

Finding the Perfect Toolkit: Analyzing Popular Python Project Templates 36

How are broad integer types implemented in Python? 48

Create a bot in Python to learn English 59

The thermal imager on the Raspberry PI 79

Finding a Free Parking Space with Python 91

Creating games on the Pygame framework | Part 1 114

Object-Oriented Programming (OOP) in Python 3 144

Conclusion 174

PYTHON FOR DATA SCIENCE

Introduction 179

DATA SCIENCE AND ITS SIGNIFICANCE 181

PYTHON BASICS 189

FUNCTIONS 213

LISTS AND LOOPS 230

Adding string data in Python 276

CONCLUSION 318

PYTHON

FOR

BEGINNERS

A crash course guide for machine learning and web programming.

Learn a computer language in easy steps with coding exercises.

JASON TEST

INTRODUCTION

Design patterns are reusable model for solving known and common problems in software architecture.

They are best described as templates for working with a specific normal situation. An architect can have a template for designing certain types of door frames, which he fit into many of his project, and a software engineer or software architect must know the templates for solving common programming tasks.

An excellent presentation of the design pattern should include:

Name

Motivating problem

Decision

Effects

Equivalent Problems

If you thought it was a rather vague concept, you would be right. For example, we could say that the following "pattern" solves all your problems:

Gather and prepare the necessary data and other resources

Make the necessary calculations and do the necessary work

Make logs of what you do

Free all resources

???

Profit

This is an example of too abstract thinking. You cannot call it a template because it is not an excellent model to solve any problem, even though it is technically applicable to any of them (including cooking dinner).

On the other hand, you may have solutions that are too specific to be called a template. For example, you may wonder if QuickSort is a template to solve the sorting problem.

This is, of course, a common program problems, and QuickSort is a good solution for it. However, it can be applied to any sorting problem with virtually no change.

Once you have this in the library and you can call it, your only real job is to make somehow your object comparable, and you don't have to deal with its entity yourself to change it to fit your specific problem.

Equivalent problems lie somewhere between these concepts. These are different problems that are similar enough that you can apply the same model to them, but are different enough that this model is significantly customized to be applicable in each case.

Patterns that can be applied to these kinds of problems are what we can meaningfully call design patterns.

Why use design patterns?

You are probably familiar with some design patterns through code writing practice. Many good programmers end up gravitating towards them, not even being explicitly trained, or they simply take them from their seniors along the way.

The motivation to create, learn, and use design patterns has many meanings. This is a way to name complex abstract concepts to provide discussion and learning.

They make communication within the team faster because someone can simply use the template name instead of calling the board. They allow you to learn from the experiences of people who were before you, and not to reinvent the wheel, going through the whole crucible of gradually improving practices on your own (and constantly cringing from your old code).

Bad decisions that are usually made up because they seem logical at first glance are often called anti-patterns. For something to be rightly called an anti-pattern, it must be reinvented, and for the same problem, there must be a pattern that solves it better.

Despite the apparent usefulness in this practice, designing patterns are also useful for learning. They introduce you to many problems that you may not have considered and allow you to think about scenarios with which you may not have had hands-on experience.

They are mandatory for training for all, and they are an excellent learning resources for all aspiring architect and developing who may be at the beginning of their careers and who have no direct experience in dealing with the various problems that the industry provides.

Python Design Patterns

Traditionally, design models have been divided into three main categories: creative, structural, and behavioral. There are other categories, such as architectural patterns or concurrency patterns, but they are beyond the scope of this article.

There are also Python-specific design patterns that are created specifically around problems that the language structure itself provides, or that solve problems in unique ways that are only resolved due to the language structure.

Generating Patterns deal with creating classes or objects. They serve to abstract the specifics of classes, so that we are less dependent on their exact implementation, or that we do not have to deal with complex constructions whenever we need them, or that we provide some special properties of the instantiation. They are very useful for reducing dependency and controlling how the user interacts with our classes.

Structural patterns deal with assembling objects and classes into larger structures while keeping these structures flexible and efficient. They, as a rule, are really useful for improving the readability and maintainability of the code, ensuring the correct separation of functionality, encapsulation, and the presence of effective minimal interfaces between interdependent things.

Behavioral patterns deal with algorithms in general and the distribution of responsibility between interacting objects. For example, they are good practice when you may be tempted to implement a naive solution, such as busy waiting, or load your classes with unnecessary code for one specific purpose, which is not the core of their functionality.

Generative Patterns

Factory

Abstract factory

Builder

Prototype

Singleton

Object pool

Structural Patterns

Adapter

Bridge

Composite

Decorator

Facade

Flyweight

Proxy

Behavioral patterns

Chain of responsibility

Command

Iterator

Mediator

Memento

Observer

State

Strategy

Visitor

Python Specific Design Patterns

Global object pattern

Prebound method pattern

Sentinel object pattern

Type Annotation in Python

First, let's answer the question: why do we need annotations in Python? In short, the answer will be this: to increase the information content of the source code and to be able to analyze it using specialized tools. One of the most popular, in this sense, is the control of variable types. Even though Python is a language with dynamic typing, sometimes there is a need for type control. According to PEP 3107, there may be the following annotation use cases:

type checking:

expansion of the IDE functionality in terms of providing information about the expected types of arguments and the type of return value for functions:

overload of functions and work with generics:

interaction with other languages:

use in predicate logical functions:

mapping of requests in databases:

marshaling parameters in RPC (remote procedure call)

Using annotations in functions

In functions, we can annotate arguments and the return value.

It may look like this:

```
def repeater (s: str, n: int) -> str:
return s * n
```

An annotation for an argument is defined after the colon after its name:

```
argument_name: annotation
```

An annotation that determines the type of the value returned by the function is indicated after its name using the characters ->

```
def function_name () -> type
```

Annotations are not supported for lambda functions
Access to function annotations Access to the annotations
Used in the function can be obtained through the annotations
attribute, in which annotations are presented in the form of a
dictionary, where the keys are attributes, and the values are
annotations. The main value to returned by the function is
stored in the record with the return key.
Contents of repeater . annotations :

{'n': int, 'return': str, 's': str}

4 programming languages to learn, even if you are a humanist

The digital age dictates its own rules. Now, knowledge of programming languages is moving from the category of "too highly specialized skill" to must have for a successful career. We have compiled for you the four most useful programming languages that will help you become a truly effective specialist.

Vba

If you constantly work in Excel and spend time on the same routine operations every day, you should consider automating them. Macros - queries in the VBA language built into Excel will help you with this. Having mastered macros, you can not only save time, but also free up time for more interesting tasks (for example, to write new macros). By the way, to automate some operations, learning VBA is not necessary - just record a few actions using the macro recorder, and you can repeat them from time to time. But it's better to learn this language: macro recordings will give you only limited functionality.

Despite its attractiveness, macros have two drawbacks. Firstly, since a macro automatically does all the actions that you would do with your hands, it seriously loads RAM (for example, if you have 50,000 lines in a document, your poor computer may not withstand macro attacks). The second - VBA as a programming language is not very intuitive, and it can be difficult for a beginner to learn it from scratch.

SQL

In order to combine data from different databases, you can use the formulas VPR and INDEX (SEARCH). But what if you have ten different databases with 50 columns of 10,000 rows each? Chances are good to make a mistake and spend too much time. Therefore, it is better to use the Access program. Like VPR, it is designed to combine data from various databases, but it does it much faster. Access automates this function, as well as quickly filters information and allows you to work in a team. In addition to Access, there are other programs for working with databases (DBMS), in most of which you can work using a simple programming language - SQL (Structured Query Language). Knowledge of SQL is one of the basic requirements for business analysts along with knowledge of Excel, so we advise you to take a closer look if you want to work in this area.

R

R is a good alternative to VBA if you want to make data processing easier. How is he good? Firstly, unlike a fellow, it is really simple and understandable even for those who have never had anything to do with programming in their life. Secondly, R is designed to work with databases and has wide functionality: it can change the structure of a document, collect data from the Internet, process statistically different types of information, build graphs, create tag clouds, etc. To work with Excel files, you will have to download special libraries, but it is most convenient to save tables from Excel in csv format and work in them. By the way, it is R that the program was written with which we make TeamRoulette in our championships. Thanks to her, we manage to scatter people on teams in five minutes instead of two hours. To learn how to work in R, first of all, download a visual and intuitive programming environment - RStudio .

Python

Python is an even more powerful and popular programming language (by the way, it really has nothing to do with python). Like R, Python has special libraries that work with Excel files, and it also knows how to collect information from the Internet (forget about manually driving data into tables!). You can write endlessly about Python, but if in a nutshell - it's a really convenient and quick tool that is worth mastering if you want to automate routine operations, develop your own algorithmic thinking and generally keep up with technical progress.

Unlike R, Python does not have one of the most convenient programming environments - here everyone is free to choose to taste. For example, we recommend IDLE, Jupyter Notebook, Spyder, for more advanced programmers - PyCharm.

You can learn how to program in Python and analyze data using it in our online course "Python. Data Analysis". The consultants from Big4 and Big3 will tell you how to work with libraries, create programs and algorithms for processing information.

Well, as it were, let's go

Well, if you (You, He, She, It, They) are reading this means we are starting our first Python lesson. Hooray (...) Today you will learn how to code. And what's more, you'll learn how to code in Python.

But to start coding you need Python. Where to get it?

Where to get Python?

But you think that now you can just sit down and cod. Well actually yes. BUT usually real hackers and programmers code in code editors. For working with Python We (I) recommend using a Jupyter Notebook or JupyterLab or Visual Studio Code. We (I) Will code in Visual Studio Code, but the other editors are no different.

Well, it's CODING time.

I'm too old for that

Everyone always writes the first code that displays "Hello World". Well, are we some kind of gifted? No, and therefore we will begin with this. In Python, the print () function is used to output text. To output "Hello World" we need to write the following:

```
1    print("Hello world!!!")
```

It's alife

Yes, you just wrote your first program. Now you are a programmer (NO).

Let's look at the structure of the print function. This function consists of the name - print, and the place where we throw what this function should output. If you want to display any text, you need to write it in quotation mark, either in single or double.

But now let's enter some text. For this, Python has an input function. To accept something, you need to write the following:

```
1    a=input()
2    print(a)
```

What does this program do for us? First we introduce something, at the moment we don't care what it is, text or numbers. After, our program displays what you wrote.

But how to make sure that we write the text before entering something? Really simple. There are two ways to do this.

```
1    print('          )
2    a=input()
3    print(a)
```

How can, but not necessary

If you run the second program you will notice that you have to enter data in the same line in which the text is written.

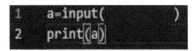

How to do

But this is not aesthetically pleasing. We are here with you all the aesthetes. And so in order for you to enter values on a separate line, you can do the following:

Like cool, but why?

As we can see, \ n appeared at the end. This is a control character that indicates the passage to the next line. But it's too lazy for me to write it down every time, and therefore I prefer to type everything in the line where the text is written.

But where to apply it? Very simple, you can take math. There are some simple arithmetic operations in Python that I will tell you about now.

Python has the following arithmetic operations: addition, subtraction, multiplication, division, integer division, exponentiation, and the remainder of division. As everything is recorded, you can see below:

```
1    6+2
2    6-2
3    6*2
4    6/2
5    3//2
6    3**2
7    3%2
```

I will finally learn how to multiply

If you want to immediately print the result, then you just need to write an arithmetic operation in print:

```
1    print(6+2)
```

The result of this program will be 8

But how do we carry out operations with numbers that the user enters? We need to use input. But by default in Python, the values that input passes are a string. And most arithmetic operations cannot be performed on a line. In order for our program to work as we intended, we need to specify what type of value Python should use.

To do this, we use the int function:

```
1    a=int(input("          : "))
2    b=int(input("          : "))
3    print(a+b)
```

We add up the two numbers that the user enters. (Wow, I found out how much 2 + 2 will be)

Python code optimization with ctypes

Content:

Basic optimizations

Styles

Python compilation

Structures in Python

Call your code in C

Pypy

Basic optimizations

Before rewriting the Python source code in C, consider the basic optimization methods in Python.

Built-in Data Structures

Python's built-in data structures, such as set and dict, are written in C. They work much faster than your own data structures composed as Python classes. Other data structures besides the standard set, dict, list, and tuple are described in the collections module documentation.

List expressions

Instead of adding items to the list using the standard method, use list expressions.

```
#Slow
    mapped = []
    for value in originallist:
    mapped.append (myfunc (value))

    # Faster
    mapped = [myfunc (value) in originallist]
```

ctypes

The ctypes module allows you to interact with C code from Python without using a module subprocessor another similar module to start other processes from the CLI.

There are only two parts: compiling C code to load in quality shared object and setting up data structures in Python code to map them to C types.

In this article, I will combine my Python code with LCS.c, which finds the longest subsequence in two-line lists. I want the following to work in Python:

```
list1 = ['My', 'name', 'is', 'Sam', 'Stevens', '!']
    list2 = ['My','name', 'is', 'Alex', 'Stevens', '.']

    common = lcs (list1, list2)

    print (common)
    # ['My', 'name', 'is', 'Stevens']
```

One problem is that this particular C function is the signature of a function that takes lists of strings as argument types and returns a type that does not have a fixed length. I solve this problem with a sequence structure containing pointers and lengths.

Compiling C code in Python

First, C source code (lcs.c) is compiled in lcs.soto load in Python.

```
gcc -c -Wall -Werror -fpic -O3 lcs.c -o lcs.o
    gcc -shared -o lcs.so lcs.o
```

Wall will display all warnings:

Werror will wrap all warnings in errors:

fpic will generate position-independent instructions that you will need if you want to use this library in Python:

O3 maximizes optimization:

And now we will begin to write Python code using the resulting shared object file.

Structures in Python

Below are two data structures that are used in my C code.

```
struct sequence
    {
        char ** items:
        int length:
    }:

    struct cell
    {
        int index:
        int length:
        struct Cell * prev:
    }:
```

And here is the translation of these structures into Python.

```python
import ctypes
    class SEQUENCE (ctypes.Structure):
        _fields_ = [('items', ctypes.POINTER (ctypes.c_char_p)),
                    ('length', ctypes.c_int)]

    class CELL (ctypes.Structure):
        pass

    CELL._fields_ = [('index', ctypes.c_int), ('length',
ctypes.c_int),
                    ('prev', ctypes.POINTER (CELL))]
```

A few notes:

All structures are classes that inherit from ctypes.Structure.

The only field _fields_is a list of tuples. Each tuple is (<variable-name>, <ctypes.TYPE>).

There ctypesare similar types in c_char (char) and c_char_p (* char) .

There is ctypesalso one POINTER()that creates a type pointer from each type passed to it.

If you have a recursive definition like in CELL, you must pass the initial declaration, and then add the fields _fields_in order to get a link to yourself later.

Since I did not use CELLPython in my code, I did not need to write this structure, but it has an interesting property in the recursive field.

Call your code in C

In addition, I needed some code to convert Python types to new structures in C. Now you can use your new C function to speed up Python code.

```python
def list_to_SEQUENCE (strlist: List [str]) -> SEQUENCE:
    bytelist = [bytes (s, 'utf-8') for s in strlist]
    arr = (ctypes.c_char_p * len (bytelist)) ()
    arr [:] = bytelist
    return SEQUENCE (arr, len (bytelist))


def lcs (s1: List [str], s2: List [str]) -> List[str]:
    seq1 = list_to_SEQUENCE(s1)
    seq2 = list_to_SEQUENCE(s2)

# struct Sequence * lcs (struct Sequence * s1, struct Sequence *
s2)
common = lcsmodule.lcs (ctypes.byref (seq1), ctypes.byref
(seq2)) [0]

    ret = []

    for i in range (common.length):
        ret.append (common.items [i] .decode ('utf-8'))
    lcsmodule.freeSequence (common)

    return ret

lcsmodule = ctypes.cdll.LoadLibrary ('lcsmodule / lcs.so')
lcsmodule.lcs.restype = ctypes.POINTER (SEQUENCE)

list1 = ['My', 'name', 'is', 'Sam', 'Stevens', '!']
list2 = ['My', 'name', 'is', 'Alex', 'Stevens', '.']

common = lcs (list1, list2)

print (common)

# ['My', 'name', 'is', 'Stevens']
```

A few notes:

**char (list of strings) matches directly to a list of bytes in Python.

There lcs.cis a function lcs()with the signature struct Sequence * lcs (struct Sequence * s1, struct Sequence s2) . To set up the return type, I use lcsmodule.lcs.restype = ctypes.POINTER(SEQUENCE).

To make a call with a reference to the Sequence structure, I use ctypes.byref()one that returns a "light pointer" to your object (faster than ctypes.POINTER()).

common.items- this is a list of bytes, they can be decoded to get retin the form of a list str.

lcsmodule.freeSequence (common) just frees the memory associated with common. This is important because the garbage collector (AFAIK) will not automatically collect it.

Optimized Python code is code that you wrote in C and wrapped in Python.

Something More: PyPy

Attention: I myself have never used PyPy.

One of the simplest optimizations is to run your programs in the PyPy runtime, which contains a JIT compiler (just-in-time) that speeds up the work of loops, compiling them into machine code

for repeated execution.

Finding the Perfect Toolkit: Analyzing Popular Python Project Templates

The materials, the translation of which we publish today, is dedicated to the story about the tools used to create Python applications. It is designed for those programmers who have already left the category of beginners but have not yet reached the category of experienced Python developers.

For those who can't wait to start practice, the author suggests using Flake8,pytest, and Sphinx in existing Python projects. He also recommends a look at pre-commit,Black, and Pylint. Those who plan to start a new project, he advises paying attention to Poetry and Dependable.

Overview

It has always been difficult for me to form an objective opinion about the "best practices" of Python development. In the world of technology, some popular trends are continually emerging, often not existing for long. This complicates the extraction of the "useful signal" from the information noise.

The freshest tools are often only good, so to speak, on paper. Can they help the practical programmer with something? Or their application only leads to the introduction of something new in the project, the performance of which must be maintained, which carries more difficulties than benefits?

I didn't have a clear understanding of what exactly I considered the "best practices" of development. I suppose I found something useful, based mainly on episodic evidence of "utility," and on the occasional mention of this in conversations. I decided to put things in order in this matter. To do this, I began to analyze all the templates of Python projects that I could find (we are talking about templates used by the cookiecutter command-line utility to create Python projects based on them).

It seemed to me that it was fascinating to learn about what auxiliary tools the template authors consider worthy of getting these tools into new Python projects created based on these templates.

I analyzed and compared the 18 most popular template projects (from 76 to 6300 stars on GitHub), paying particular attention to what kind of auxiliary tools they use. The results of this examination can be found in this table.

Below I want to share the main conclusions that I have made while analyzing popular templates.

De facto standards

The tools discussed in this section are included in more than half of the templates. This means that they are perceived as standard in a large number of real Python projects.

Flake8

I have been using Flake8 for quite some time, but I did not know about the dominant position in the field of linting that this tool occupies. I thought that it exists in a kind of competition, but the vast majority of project templates use it.

Yes, this is not surprising. It is difficult to oppose something to the convenience of linting the entire code base of the project in a matter of seconds. Those who want to use cutting-edge development can recommend a look at us make-python-style guide. This is something like "Flake8 on steroids." This tool may well contribute to the transfer to the category of obsolete other similar tools (like Pylint).

Pytest and coverage.py

The vast majority of templates use pytest. This reduces the use of the standard unit test framework. Pytest looks even more attractive when combined with tox. That's precisely what was done in about half of the templates. Code coverage with tests is most often checked using coverage.py.

Sphinx

Most templates use Sphinx to generate documentation. To my surprise, MkDocs is rarely used for this purpose.

As a result, we can say that if you do not use Flake8, pytest, and Sphinx in your current project, then you should consider introducing them.

Promising tools

In this section, I collected those tools and techniques, the use of which in the templates suggested some trends. The point is that although all this does not appear in most project templates, it is found in many relatively recent templates. So - all this is worth paying attention to.

Pyproject.toml

File usage is pyproject.tomlsuggested in PEP 518. This is a modern mechanism for specifying project assembly requirements. It is used in most fairly young templates.

Poetry

Although the Python ecosystem isn't doing well in terms of an excellent tool for managing dependencies, I cautiously optimistic that Poetry could be the equivalent of npm from the JavaScript world in the Python world.

The youngest (but popular) project templates seem to agree with this idea of mine. Real, it is worth saying that if someone is working on some kind of library that he can plan to distribute through PyPI, then he will still have to use setup tools. (It should to be noted that after the publication of this material, I was informed that this is no longer a problem).

Also, be careful if your project (the same applies to dependencies) relies on Conda. In this case, Poetry will not suit you, since this tool, in its current form, binds the developer to pip and virtualenv.

Dependabot

Dependabot regularly checks project dependencies for obsolescence and tries to help the developer by automatically opening PR.

I have recently seen this tool more often than before. It seems like to me that it is an excellent tool: the addition of which to the project affects the project very positively. Dependabot helps reduce security risks by pushing developers to keep dependencies up to date.

As a result, I advised you not to lose sight of Poetry and Dependabot. Consider introducing these tools into your next project.

Personal recommendations

Analysis of project templates gave me a somewhat ambivalent perception of the tools that I will list in this section. In any case, I want to use this section to tell about them, based on my own experience. At one time, they were beneficial to me.

Pre-commit

Even if you are incredibly disciplined - do not waste your energy on performing simple routine actions such as additional code run through the linter before sending the code to the repository. Similar tasks can be passed to Pre-commit. And it's better to spend your energy on TDD and teamwork on code.

Pylint

Although Pylint is criticized for being slow, although this tool is criticized for the features of its settings, I can say that it allowed me to grow above myself in the field of programming.
He gives me specific instructions on those parts of the code that I can improve, tells me how to make the code better comply with the rules. For a free tool, this alone is already very much. Therefore, I am ready to put up with the inconvenience associated with Pylint.

Black

Black at the root of the debate over where to put spaces in the code. This protects our teams from an empty talk and meaningless differences in files caused by different editors' settings.

In my case, it brightens up what I don't like about Python (the need to use a lot of spaces). Moreover, it should be noted that the Black project in 2019 joined the Python Software Foundation, which indicates the seriousness and quality of this project.

As a result, I want to say that if you still do not use pre-commit, Black, and Pylint - think about whether these tools can benefit your team.

Subtotals

Twelve of the eighteen investigated templates were created using the cookiecutter framework. Some of those templates where this framework is not used have exciting qualities.

But given the fact that cookiecutter is the leading framework for creating project templates, those who decide to use a template that did not use a cookiecutter should have excellent reasons for this. Such a decision should be very well justified.

Those who are looking for a template for their project should choose a template that most closely matches his view of things. If you, when creating projects according to a precise template, continuously have to reconfigure them in the same way, think about how to fork such a template and refine it, inspired by examples of templates from my list.

And if you are attracted to adventure - create your template from scratch. Cookiecutter is an excellent feature of the Python ecosystem, and the simple process of creating Jinja templates allows you to quickly and easily do something your own.

Bonus: Template Recommendations

Django

Together with the most popular Django templates, consider using we make-django-template. It gives the impression of a deeply thought out product.

Data Processing and Analysis

In most projects aimed at processing and analyzing data, the Cookiecutter Data Science template is useful. However, data scientists should also look at Kedro.

This template extends Cookiecutter Data Science with a mechanism for creating standardized data processing pipelines. It supports loading and saving data and models. These features are very likely to be able to find a worthy application in your next project.

Here I would also like to express my gratitude to the creators of the shablona template for preparing very high- quality documentation. It can be useful to you even if you end up choosing something else.

General Purpose Templates

Which general-purpose template to choose in some way depends on what exactly you are going to develop based on this template - a library or a regular application. But I, selecting a similar template, along with the most popular projects of this kind, would look very closely at Jace's Python Template.

This is not a well-known pattern, but I like the fact that it has Poetry, isort , Black, pylint, and mypy .

PyScaffold is one of the most popular non-cookiecutter based templates. It has many extensions (for example, for Django, and Data Science projects). It also downloads version numbers from GitHub using setuptools-scm. Further, this is one of the few templates supporting Conda.

Here are a couple of templates that use GitHub Actions technology:

The Python Best Practices Cookiecutter template, which, I want to note, has most of my favorite tools.

The Blueprint / Boilerplate For Python Projects template, which I find pretty interesting, as the ability it gives them to find common security problems with Bandit, looks promising. Also, this template has a remarkable feature, which consists in the fact that the settings of all tools are collected in a single file setup.cfg.

And finally - I recommend taking a look at we make-python-package template. I think it's worth doing it anyway. In particular, if you like the Django template of the same developer, or if you are going to use the advanced, we make-python-style guide instead of pure Flake8.

How are broad integer types implemented in Python?

When you write in a low-level language such as C, you are worried about choosing the right data type and qualifiers for your integers, at each step, you analyze whether it will be enough to use it simply intor whether you need to add longor even long double. However, when writing code in Python, you don't need to worry about these "minor" things, because Python can work with numbers of integerany size type .

In C, if you try to calculate 220,000 using the built-in function

```
#include <stdio.h>
#include <math.h>

int main (void) {
    printf ("%Lf\n", powl (2, 20000)):
    return 0:
}

$ ./a.out
inf
```

powl, you will get the output inf.

But in Python, making this easier than ever is easy:

```
>>> 2 ** 20,000
398027684033796659235430720619120245370477278049242593871134 ...

... 6021 digits long ...

6309376
```

It must be under the hood that Python is doing something very beautiful, and today we will find out the exactly what it does to work with integers of arbitrary size!

Presentation and Definition

Integer in Python, this is a C structure defined as follows:

```
struct _longobject {
    PyObject_VAR_HEAD
    digit ob_digit [1];
};
PyObject_VAR_HEADIs a macro, it expands to PyVarObject, which has the following structure:
typedef struct {
    PyObject ob_base;
    Py_ssize_t ob_size; /* Number of items in variable part */
} PyVarObject;
```

Other types that have PyObject_VAR_HEAD:

PyBytesObject

PyTupleObject

PyListObject

This means that an integer, like a tuple or a list, has a variable length, and this is the first step to understanding how Python can support work with giant numbers. Once expanded, the macro _longobjectcan be considered as:

```
struct _longobject {
    PyObject ob_base;
    Py_ssize_t ob_size; /* Number of items in variable part */
    digit ob_digit [1];
};
```

There PyObjectare some meta fields in the structure that are used for reference counting (garbage collection), but to talk about this, we need a separate article. The field on which we will focus this ob_digitand in a bit ob_size.

Decoding ob_digit

ob_digitIs a statically allocated array of unit length of type digit (typedef для uint32_t). Since this is an array, it ob_digitis a pointer primarily to a number, and therefore, if necessary, it can be increased using the malloc function to any length. This way, python can represent and process very large numbers.

Typically, in low-level languages such as C, the precision of integers is limited to 64 bits. However, Python supports integers of arbitrary precision. Starting with Python 3, all numbers are presented in the form bignum and are limited only by the available system memory.

Decoding ob_size

ob_sizestores the number of items in ob_digit. Python overrides and then uses the value ob_sizeto to determine the actual number of elements contained in the array to increase the efficiency of allocating memory to the array ob_digit.

Storage

The most naive way to store integer numbers is to store one decimal digit in one element of the array. Operation such as additional and subtractions can be performed according to the rules of mathematics from elementary school.

With this approach, the number 5238 will be saved like this:
This approach is inefficient because we will use up to 32-bit digits (uint32_t) for storing a decimal digit, which ranges from 0 to 9 and can be easily represented with only 4 bits. After all, when writing something as universal like python, the kernel developer needs to be even more inventive.

So, can we do better? Of course, otherwise, we would not have posted this article. Let's take a closer look at how Python stores an extra-long integer.

Python path

Instead of storing only one decimal digit in each element of the array ob_digit, Python converts the numbers from the number system with base 10 to the numbers in the system with base 230 and calls each element as a number whose value ranges from 0 to 230 - 1.

In the hexadecimal number system, the base 16 ~ 24 means that each "digit" of the hexadecimal number ranges from 0 to 15 in the decimal number system. In Python, it's similar to a "number" with a base of 230, which means that the number will range from 0 to 230 - 1 = 1073741823 in decimal.

In this way, Python effectively uses almost all of the allocated space of 32 bits per digit, saves resources, and still performs simple operations, such as adding and subtracting at the math level of elementary school.

Depending on the platform, Python uses either 32-bit unsigned integer arrays or 16-bit unsigned integer arrays with 15-bit digits. To perform the operations that will be discussed later, you need only a few bits.

Example: 1152921504606846976

As already mentioned, for Python, numbers are represented in a system with a base of 230, that is, if you convert 1152921504606846976 into a number system with a base of 230, you will get 100.

1152 9215 0460 6846 976 = 1 * ((230) 2 + 0) * ((230) 1 + 0) *((230) 0)

Since it is the ob_digitfirst to store the least significant digit, it is stored as 001 in three digits. The structure _longobjectfor this value will contain:

ob_size like 3

ob_digit like [0, 0, 1]

We created a demo REPL that will show how Python stores an integer inside itself, and also refers to structural members such as ob_size, ob_refcountetc.

Integer Long Operations

Now that we have a pure idea of how Python implements integers of arbitrary precision, it is time to understand how various mathematical operations are performed with them.

Addition

Integers are stored "in numbers," which means that addition is as simple as in elementary school, and the Python source code shows us that this is how addition is implemented. A function with a name x_addin a file longobject.cadds two numbers.

```
For (i = 0; i < size_b; ++i) {
    carry += a-> ob_digit [i] + b-> ob_digit [i];
    z-> ob_digit [i] = carry & PyLong_MASK;
    carry >> = PyLong_SHIFT;
}
For ( i < size_a; ++i) {
    carry += a-> ob_digit [i];
    z-> ob_digit [i] = carry & PyLong_MASK;
    carry >> = PyLong_SHIFT;
}
z-> ob_digit [i] = carry;
```

The code snippet above is taken from a function x_add. As you can see, it iterates over a number by numbers and performs the addition of numbers, calculates the result and adds hyphenation.

It becomes more interesting when the result of addition is a negative number. The sign ob_sizeis an integer sign, that is, if you have a negative number, then it ob_sizewill be a minus. The value ob_sizemodulo will determine the number of digits in ob_digit.

Subtraction

Just as addition takes place, subtraction also takes place. A function with a name x_subin the file longobject.csubtracts one number from another.

```
For (i = 0; i < size_b; ++i) {
    borrow = a->ob_digit [i] - b->ob_digit [i] - borrow;
    z->ob_digit [i] = borrow & PyLong_MASK;
    borrow >> = PyLong_SHIFT;
    borrow & = 1; /* Keep only one sign bit */
}
for (; i <size_a; ++i) {
    borrow = a->ob_digit [i] - borrow;
    z->ob_digit [i] = borrow & PyLong_MASK;
    borrow >> = PyLong_SHIFT;
    borrow & = 1; /* Keep only one sign bit */
}
```

The code snippet above is taken from a function x_sub. In it, you see how the enumeration of numbers occurs and subtraction is performed, the result is calculated and the transfer is distributed. Indeed, it is very similar to addition.

Multiplication

And again, the multiplication will be implemented in the same naive way that we learned from the lessons of mathematics in elementary school, but it is not very efficient. To maintain efficiency, Python implements theKaratsuba algorithm, which multiplies two n-digit numbers in O (nlog23) simple steps. The algorithm is not simple and its implementation is beyond the scope of this article, but you can find its implementation in functions and in the file .k_mul k_lopsided_mullongobject.c

Division and other operations

All operations on integers are defined in the file longobject.c, they are very simple to find and trace the work of each. Attention: A detailed understanding of the work of each of them will take time, so pre-stock up with popcorn.

Optimizing Frequently Used Integers

Python preallocates a small number of integers in memory ranging from -5 to 256. This allocation occurs during initialization, and since we cannot change integers (immutability), these pre-allocated numbers are singleton and are directly referenced instead of being allocated. This means that every time we use/create a small number, Python instead of reallocation simply returns a reference to the previously allocated number.

Such optimization can be traced in the macro IS_SMALL_INTand function get_small_intc longobject.c. So Python saves a lot of space and time in calculating commonly used integer numbers.

Create a bot in Python to learn English

No, this is not one of the hundreds of articles on how to write your first Hello World bot in Python. Here you will not find detailed instructions on how to get an API token in BotFather or launch a bot in the cloud. In return, we will show you how to unleash the full power of Python to the maximum to achieve the most aesthetic and beautiful code. We perform a song about the appeal of complex structures - we dance and dance. Under the cut asynchrony, its system of saves, a bunch of useful decorators, and a lot of beautiful code.

Disclaimer: People with brain OOP and adherents of the "right" patterns may ignore this article.

Idea

To understand what it is like not to know English in modern society, imagine that you are an 18th-century nobleman who does not know French. Even if you are not very well versed in history, you can still imagine how hard it would be to live under such circumstances. In the modern world, English has become a necessity, not a privilege, especially if you are in the IT industry. The project is based on the catechism of the future: the development of a neural network as a separate unit, and education, which is based on games and sports spirit. Isomorphic paradigms have been hanging in the air since ancient times, but it seems that over time, people began to forget that the most straightforward solutions are the most effective.

Here is a shortlist of the basic things I want to put together:

Be able to work with three user dictionaries

Ability to parse youtube video/text, and then add new words to the user's dictionary

Two basic skills training modes

Flexible customization: full control over user dictionaries and the environment in general

Built-in admin panel

Naturally, everything should work quickly, with the ability to easily replenish existing functionality in the future. Putting it all together, I thought that the best embodiment of my idea into reality would be a Telegram bot. My tale is not about how to write handlers for the bot correctly - there are dozens of such articles, and this is simple mechanical work. I want the reader to learn to ignore the typical dogmas of programming. Use what is profitable and effective here and now.

"I learned to let out the cries of unbelievers past my ears because it was impossible to suppress them."

Base structure

The bot will be based on the python-telegram-bot (ptb) library. I use loguru as a logger , though there is one small snag here. The fact is that ptb by default uses a different logger (standard logging) and does not allow you to connect your own. Of course, it would be possible to intercept all journal messages globally and send them to our registrar, but we will do it a little easier:

```
from loguru import logger
import sys

# Configure dual-stream output to the console and to the file
config = {
    'handlers': [
        {'sink': sys.stdout, 'level': 'INFO'},
        {'sink': 'logs.log', 'serialize': False, 'level': 'DEBUG'},
    ]
}

logger.configure(** config)

# ...

updater = Updater('YOUR_TOKEN')
dp = updater.dispatcher

# Roughly fasten your logger. Cheap and cheerful
updater.logger = logger
dp.logger = logger
```

Unfortunately, I don't have the opportunity to deploy my bot on stable data centers, so data security is a priority. For these purposes, I implemented my system of saves. It provides flexible and convenient work with data - statistics collection, as an example of easy replenishment of functionality in the future.

```python
from __future__ import annotations # In the future, I will omit this import
from loguru import logger

import inspect
import functools
import os

def file_is_empty (path: str) -> bool:
    return os.stat (path) .st_size == 0

def clear_file (path: str) -> None:
    with open (path, 'w'): pass

def cache_decorator (method):
    @ functools.wraps (method)
    def wrapper (self, * args, ** kwargs):
        res = method (self, * args, ** kwargs)
        Cache.link.recess (self, {'method_name': method __ name__}) # (1)
        # During testing, multiple calls can slow down
        # program work: opt avoids this
        logger.opt (lazy = True) .debug (f'Decorator for {method __ name__} was end ')
        return res
    return wrapper

class cache:
    " "
```

+ cache_si ze - Std thfDtlgh 'hi ch dl data will be su'ed

+ cache_files - Dump file in w'hich all intermediate operations on

data are stored

link = None

def   init   (self. cache_si ze =10):

= Save all screw'ed cl asses. Thi s all or's you t o fl exibl·' vork with

data.

sel f. cl asses = []

=Files matching classes

 sel f._cache_fi1es = []

= (1). A sm dl hack that dl or's you to cd1 a specifi c instance

thrDtlgh a common class

= Thi s w'wks because w'e oril \' have one instance Df the cl ass. 'hi ch

= implements d 1 the logic of 'orking with data. In additi on. it is
convenient ari d all o 's
= st gum cantl>' expand the functl Dflallt>' in the future
sel f. cl ass .link = self

self._counter = 0
self.CACHE SIZE = cache st ze
def add (self, d s: class, file: str) -> NDne:

All or's to fasten a class to a sa ver

+ cls - Inst an ce of the class
+ file - The fi1 e the instari ce is 'orking with

self._cache_files.append (file)
self._cl asses.append (cls)

if fi1e i s eotptl' (fi1e): return hDne

1ogger.opt dan.'=True).debug(fTor{cls.   class names) file (file)
is not empty' ')

fa data in sells oad(file):
    is.save nDn Caclti ng (data)

```python
cl ear_file (file)
sel f._counter = 0


def recess (self, cls: ct ass, data diet) —>Ncri e:

    The main method that performs the basi c l o c of saves

    if self. counter + 1/ = self.CACHE SIZE:
            self.save all 0
    el se:
    self._counter + = I
    fil ename = self._cache_files [self._classes.index (cls)]
    self.save (data. fil enam e = filename)


= For simplicit›', save_d1, save, load methods are omitted
```

Now we can create any methods that can modify data, without fear of losing important data:

```python
@cache_decorator
def add_smth_important (* args, ** kwargs) -> Any:
    # ...
    # We make some important actions on the data ...
    # ...
```

Now that we have figured out the basic structure, the main question remains: how to put everything together. I implemented the main class - EnglishBot, which brings together the entire primary structure: PTB, work with the database, the save system, and which will manage the whole business logic of the bot. If the implementation of Telegram commands were simple, we could easily add them to the same class. But, unfortunately, their organization occupies most of the code of the entire application, so adding them to the same class would be crazy. I also did not want to create new classes/subclasses, because I suggest using a very simple structure:

```
# Import the main class
from modules import EnglishBot
# Import classes that implement Telegram commands
from modules.module import start
# ...

if __name__ == '__main__':
    # Initialize the bot
    tbot = EnglishBot (
        # ...
    )

    # Add handlers to the stack
    tbot.add_command_handler (start, 'start')
    # ...
```

How command modules get access to the main class, we will consider further.

All out of nothing

Ptb handlers have two arguments - update and context, which store all the necessary information stack. Context has a wonderful chat_data argument that can be used as a data storage dictionary for chat. But I do not want to constantly refer to it in a format context.chat_data['data']. I would like something

light and beautiful, say context.data. However, this is not a
problem.

```python
from telegram.ext import CommandHandler

def a (self, key: str):
    # First, check if the class has the required value
    # If not, then try to return it from chat_data
    try:
        return object __getattribute__ (self, key)
    except:
        return self.chat_data [key]

def b (self, key: str, data = None, replace = True):
    #Small hack: if replace = False and data exists, then overwriting does not occur
    # In this case, if the data is not specified, then they are put in None
    if replace or not self.chat_data.get (key, None):
        self.chat_data [key] = data

# Bindtin context to receive data in the format context.data
CallbackContext __getattribute__ = a
# As well as a convenient setter for your needs
CallbackContext.set = b
```

We continue to simplify our lives. Now I want all the necessary
information for a specific user to be in quick access context.

```python
def bind_context (func):
    def wrapper (update, context):
        context _bot.bind_user_data (update, context) # (2)
        return func (update, context)
    return wrapper

class EnglishBot:
    # ...

    def bind_user_data (self, update, context) -> dict:
        context.set ('t_id', update.message.chat_id, replace = False)
        context.set ('t_ln', update.message.from_user.language_code, replace = False)
        # ...
        # Set all the necessary information that we want to have quick access from context
        # For example, something from the database
        # ...
```

Now we'll completely become impudent and fasten our bot
instance to context:

```python
class EnglishBot:
    # ...

    def __init__ (self, * args, ** kwargs):
        # ...
        # (2): Now we can access the instance in the format context._bot
        CallbackContext._bot = self
```

We put everything in place and get a citadel of comfort and convenience in just one call.

```
from EnglishBot import bind_context

@bind_context
def start (update, context):
    # Now we have access to everything from one place
    # For example, we can easily add a new user to the database
    # Check if the user is in our database
    if not context._bot.user_exist (context.t_id):
        # For example, add some important notifications
        context.set ('push_notification', True)
        # And then add the user to the database
        context._bot.new_user (context.t_id, context.t_ln)

    return update.message.reply_text ('Welcome')
    # ...
```

Decorators are our everything

Most often, it turns out that the name of the function coincides with the name of the command to which we want to add a handler. Why not use this statistical feature for your selfish purposes.

```
class EnglishBot:
    # ...

    def add_command_handler (self, func: function, name = None) -> None:
        """
        Function that adds a command handler
        """

        name = name or func.__name__
        self.dp.add_handler (CommandHandler (name, func))

    # ...

# In the main file:
tbot.add_command_handler (start) # Instead of tbot.add_command_handler (start, 'start')
```

It looks cool, but it doesn't work. It's all about the bind_context decorator, which will always return the name of the wrapper function. Correct this misunderstanding.

```python
import functools

def bind_context (func):
    # functools.wraps from stdlib saves signatures since Python 3.4
    @ functools.wraps (func)
    def wrapper (update, context):
        context._bot.bind_user_data (update, context)
        return func (update, context)
    return wrapper
```

There are many message handlers in the bot, which, by design, should cancel the command when entering zero. Also I need to discard all edited posts.

```python
import functools

END = -1

def zero_exiter (func):
    @ functools.wraps (func)
    def wrapper (update, context):
        if update.to_dict () ['message']. get ('text', None) == '0':
            update.message.reply_text ('Sending some message')
            return END

        return func (update, context)
    return wrapper

def skip_edited (func):
    @ functools.wraps (func)
    def wrapper (update, context):
        # This works in all cases, because None returned
        # in the conversation_handler stack, leaves the function in its current state
        if not update.to_dict (). get ('edited_message', None):
            return func (update, context)
    return wrapper
```

We do not forget at the same time about the most important decorator - @run_asyncon which asynchrony is based. Now we collect the heavy function.

```python
from telegram.ext.dispatcher import run_async
from EnglishBot import skip_edited

@run_async
@skip_edited
def heavy_function (update, context):
    # ...
    # A heavy computing function that needs asynchrony
    # Has post edit protection
    # ...
```

Remember that asynchrony is a Jedi sword, but with this sword, you can quickly kill yourself.

Sometimes programs freeze without sending anything to the log. @logger.catch, the last decorator on our list, ensures that any error is correctly reported to a logger.

```python
from loguru import logger

@logger.catch
def heavy_function2 (update, context):
    # ...
    # Another heavy computing function on which a program may hang
    # ...
```

Admin panel

Let's implement an admin panel with the ability to receive/delete logs and send a message to all users.

```python
from EnglishBot import bind_context
from Cache import file_is_empty
from telegram import ReplyKeyboardMarkup
from loguru import logger

LOG_FILE = 'logs.log'
SENDING, MAIN, END = range (1, -2, -1)

buttons = ReplyKeyboardMarkup (
    [('Get logs', 'logs'), ('Clear logs', 'clear')],
    [('Send message', 'send')],
    # [...],
)

@bind_context
def admin_panel (update, context):
    # Check user admin rights
    if not context._bot.acess_check (context1.id):
        # A good security practice is to show the user that such a command does not exist
        return update.message.reply_text (f'Unknown command {update.message.text} ')

    update.message.reply_text ('Choose an option', reply_markup = buttons)

    return MAIN
```

!fi ero exiter
def send d1 (updast   context).
    count = 0

!fi ero exiter
def send d1 (updast   context).
    count = 0

```
def get logs (update context).
    if fil e is empU.' (LOG FILE).
        update.cd1back quo.'.rep1ɔ' text
            are empU.") else.
        = Show' document loading
        context.bot.send chat acti ɔxi
        (chat id = context.t icL action
        = 'upload docum cut')
        context.bot.sendDocument (chat i
        d = context.t icL docimi cut =
        open (L OG FILE 'rb') name = L
        Ohr FILE
time‹xit = 1000)
```

> = Since we do not cl ose the admin
> panel you need to rem ove the
> dourload icon on the button
> update.cd1back quell'.answer (text
> = ")

> = B asicd1\' thi s is urin ecessm.'. As I
> sai d earli er None does not change the
> positi on of the hand er

> = But this was' the code locks much
> m‹xe readabl e return ñIAIN

```
def logs d ear (update context).
    with open (LOG FILE 'u") as fil e.
        update.cd1back quo.'.rep1ɔ' text
        ('O ear ed) update.cd1back
        quo.'.answer (text = ")

    return ñIAIN
```

= Send methods

```
def take message (update context).
    update.cd1back quell'.rep1ɔ' text
    ('Send m essag e) update.cd1back
    quell'.answer (text = ")

    return SENDING
```

```
!fi ero exiter
def send d1 (updast    context).
    count = 0
```

Get user identifi cfs from the
database for id in li st (context.
bot.get user ids Q).
= It may' happen that some user
has added a bet to the em ergenc\'
= Then when to.'ing to send him a
message an error u411 be caught
to.'.
= fi'e do not setid a message to
oursel ves if i d   context.t icL
continue
= Be sure to use ñlarkdour to
save message formatting
context.bet.send message
(context.t icL text =
update.message.text markdour
parse mode = ñlarkdour')
count + = 1
except. pass

update.cd1back quell'.rep1>' text
(£Sent to { count) pecpl e ')
update.cd1back quell'.answer (text
= ")

```
#....

# In the main file.
tbot.add_conversation_handler (
    entry_points = [('admin', admin)].
    # The regularity for send_alk allows you to process any message that does not start with /
    states = [[(logs, " logs $'), (logs_clear, " clear $'), (send, " send $')], [(send_alk, "@ ^ ((?!, * (( ^ \/) +)). *)( +)$
')]]
)
```

The add_conversation_handler function allows you to add a

conversation handler in a minimalistic way:

```python
class EnglishBot:
    # ...

    def add_conversation_handler (self, entry_points: list, states: list, fallbacks: list) -> None:
        fallbacks = [CommandHandler (name, func) for name, func in fallbacks]
        entry_points = [CommandHandler (name, func) for name, func in entry_points]
        r_states = {}

        for i in range (len (states)):
            r_states [i] = []

            # Each array describes functions of one state
            for func, pattern in states [i]:
                # If the regular starts with the @ symbol, then we add a message handler
                # Otherwise, a regular button handler
                if pattern [0] == '@':
                    r_states [i] .append (MessageHandler (Filters.regex (pattern [1:]), func))
                else:
                    r_states [i] .append (CallbackQueryHandler (func, pattern = pattern))

        conv_handler = ConversationHandler (entry_points = entry_points, states = r_states, fallbacks = fallbacks)
        dp.add_handler (conv_handler)
```

Main functionality

Let's teach our bot to add new words to user dictionaries.

```python
from EnglishBot import bind_context, skip_edited, zero_exiter
from youtube_transcript_api import YouTubeTranscriptApi
from telegram.ext.dispatcher import run_async

START_OVER, ADDING, END = range (1, -2, -1)

re_youtube = re.compile ('^ (http (s)?: \/\/)? ((w) {3}.)? youtu (be | .be)? (\. com)? \/.+' )
re_text = re.compile ('^ [a-z] {3,20} $')

def is_youtube_link (link: str) -> bool:
    if re_youtube.match (link) is not None: return True

def clear_text (text: str) -> str:
    bad_symbols = '! @ #% $ ^ & * () _ + 1234567890 -= /| \\?> <., ":: ~ [] {}'
```

```python
        text = text.replace (s. ")

    return  text.stra⁄   ()  1DS`& ()

!@skip_edited
:@bind_context
def add_w'ords (update. context).
    update.message.reply' text ('Enter text:')
    return ADDING

:H uri_asx'nc
:@skip_edit ed
:@zero_exiter
def parse_text (update. context):
    DDDM DZténg takes soote titzte, sD ñ'ou need tD T1ctT 1' the user that e\' .'thing is fine
    message = update.message.repl»'_text ('L oad rig ...')

    if is 'outube_link (update.message.text):
      = If the video is irivdid or there are no subtitl es in it, then we will catch ari  error
      to.':
            transcript list = Y en TubeTranscriptApi list transcripts (get ski deD id (update.message.text))
            t = tr ariscript_listfnd_transcript (['en'])
            _tmt = clear_tmt  ('.' .j » ([i [tmt'] fur i in tletJ  0])}  split ()
        except:
            otessag z edtt text ('k\'âtid x'ideD. To.' again:')
            return ADD UG
    else:
        _text = clear_tnt (update.message.text) .split ()

  =  ¥Ve get  a link to the words the user  alread>' has
    T'&ds.'  CDotext.  bDt.get ck ct  'ords (cDlttWt.t id)
    l 'ards tD be ad6ed
    good_w'ords = []
  = Discarded words
    bad_words = Q

  = First, w'e discard duplicates
    for word in set   text):
      =  Then  w'e check the correctness of the w'ord regular
        z = re_text.match (word)
        if z.
          = Add a vord onl>' if it is n ot already' in the user ñ ation m.'
            if z.group () net in _w'ords:
                good_wcrds.append (word)
        el se:
            bad_words.append ('ord)

  = The Dnl >' thi Hg left 1 S tD suggest the user tD Add ends
  = And then add them t o the di cti Dfl .'
```

.. In the main file:

```
tbot.add_coriversation_handler (
    entr)'  oints = [('add_wcrds', add_ 'crds)],
```

```
states = [
    [(parse_text, '@ ^ ((?). * ((^ \ /) +)). *)( . +) $9].
    # ...
])
```

We pack the bot

Before we pack our bot, add proxy support and change log levels
from the console.

```
# In the main file:

import argparse

parser = argparse.ArgumentParser ()
parser.add_argument ('- l', '--level', default = 'INFO',
            choices = ['TRACE', 'DEBUG', 'INFO', 'SUCCESS', 'WARNING', 'ERROR', 'CRITICAL'],
            help = 'Allows you to enable the bot in a given mode')
parser.add_argument ('- p', '--proxy', help = 'Allows you to enable bot with proxy')
args = parser.parse_args ()

config = {
   handlers: [
      {'sink': sys.stdout, 'level': args.level},
      # It's not a mistake. In the file I collect logs of level DEBUG and higher
      {'sink': logs.log', 'serialize': False, 'level': DEBUG'},
   ],
}

logger.configure (** config)

if args.proxy:
    t_proxy = {'proxy_url': args.proxy, 'read_timeout': 1000, 'connect_timeout': 1000}
    # ...
    # Proxies for other services
    # ...
else:
    t_proxy = None
```

Python 3.5+ supports the ability to pack a directory into a single
executable file. Let's take this opportunity to be able to deploy
your work environment on any VPS easily. First, get the
dependency file. If you are using a virtual environment, it can be
done with one command: pip freeze > requirements.txt. If the

project does not have a virtual environment, then you will have to tinker a bit. You can try to use pip freeze and manually isolate all the necessary packages. Still, if too many packages are installed on the system, then this method will not work. The second option is to use ready-made solutions, for example, pipreqs.

Now that our dependency file is ready, we can pack our directory into a .pyzfile. To do this, enter the command py - m zipapp "ПУТЬ_К_КАТАЛОГУ" -m "ИМЯ_ГЛАВНОГО_ФАЙЛА:ГЛАВНАЯ_ФУНКЦИЯ" -o bot.pyz, it will create the bot.pyz file in the project folder. Please note that the code in init .py must be wrapped in some function, otherwise the executable file will be impossible to compile.

```
# Sample __init__.py file
# py -m zipapp "PATH_TO_CATALOG" -m "__init__.py:main" -o bot.pyz

def main ():
    #...

if __name__ == "__main__":
    main ()
```

We wrap the files in the archive zip bot.zip requirements.txt bot.pyzand send it to our VPS.

The thermal imager on the Raspberry PI

Well-known thermal imaging modules appeared on the famous Chinese site. Is it possible to assemble an exotic and, possibly, even useful thing - a home-made thermal imager? Why not, like Raspberry was lying somewhere. What came of it – I will tell you under the cut.

MLX90640. What is it?

And this, in fact, is a thermal imaging matrix with a microcontroller on board. Production of the previously unknown company Melexis. The thermal imaging matrix has a dimension of 32 by 24 pixels. This is not much, but when interpolating the image, it seems to be enough to make out something, at least.

There are two type of sensor is available version, the cases of which differ in the viewing angle of the matrix. A more squat structure A overlooks the outside world at an angle of 110 (horizontal) at 75 (vertical) degrees. B - under 55 by 37.5 degrees, respectively. The device case has only four outputs - two for power, two for communicating with the control device via the I2C interface. Interested datasheets can be downloaded here.

And then what is the GY-MCU90640?

Chinese comrades put the MLX90640 on board with another microcontroller on board (STM32F103). Apparently, for easier matrix management. This whole farm is called GY-MCU90640. And it costs at the time of acquisition (end of December 2018) in the region of 5 thousands $. As follows:

As you see, there are two types of boards, with a narrow or wide-angle version of the sensor onboard.

Which version is best for you? A good question, unfortunately, I had it only after the modules was already ordered and received. For some reason, at this time of the orders, I did not pay attention to these nuances. But in vain.

A wider version will be useful on self-propelled robots or in security system (the field of view will be larger). According to the datasheets, it also has less noise and higher measurement accuracy.

But for visualization tasks, I would more recommend a more "long-range" version of B. For one very significant reason. In the future, when shooting, it can be deployed (manually or on a platform with a drive) and take composite "photos," thereby increasing the more than a modest resolution of 32 by 24 pixels. Collects thermal images 64 by 96 pixels, for example. Well, all right, in the future, the photos will be from the wide-angle version A.

Connect to Raspberry PI

There are two ways to control the thermal imaging module: Shorten the "SET" jumper on the board and use I2C to contact the internal microcontroller MLX90640 directly.

Leave the jumper alone and communicate with the module through a similar interface installed on the STM32F103 board via RS-232.

If you write in C ++, it will probably be more convenient to ignore the extra microcontroller, short-circuit the jumper and use the API from the manufacturer, which lies here.

Humble pythonists can also go the first way. It seems like that there are a couple of Python libraries (here and here). But unfortunately, not a single one worked for me.

Advanced pythonists can write a module control driver in Python. The procedure for obtaining a frame is described in detail in the datasheet. But then you will have to prescribe all the calibration procedures, which seems slightly burdensome.

Therefore, I had to go the second way. It turned out to be moderately thorny, but quite passable.

Thanks to the insight of Chinese engineers or just a happy coincidence, the shawl turned out to have a perfect location of the conclusions:

It remains only to put the block and insert the scarf into the raspberry connector. A 5 to 3 Volt converter is installed on the board, so it seems that nothing threatens Raspberry's delicate Rx and Tx terminals.

It should be added that the connection according to the first option, is also possible, but requires more labor and solder skill. The board must be installed on the other side of the Raspberry connector (shown in the title photo of this post).

Soft

On a well-known Chinese site, such a miracle is offered to access the GY-MCU90640:

Most likely, there should be some description of the interaction protocol with the microcontroller installed on the board, according to which this software product works! After a brief conversation with the seller of scarves (respect to these respected gentlemen), such a protocol was sent to me. It appeared in pdf and pure Chinese.

Thanks to Google's translator and active copy-paste, after about an hour and a half, the protocol was decrypted, anyone can read it on Github. It turned out that the scarf understands six basic commands, among which there is a frame request on the COM port.

Each pixel of the matrix is, in fact, the temperature value of the object that this pixel is looking at. The temperature in degrees Celsius times 100 (double-byte number). There is even a special mode in which the scarf will send frames from the matrix to the Raspberry 4 times per second.

```
import numpy as np
import cv2
```

d function to get Emissivity from MCU

```
def get_emissivity ():
```

```python
ser.write (semi d .to_bytes ([0xA5,Dx55 ,0xOI ,OxFB]))
read = ser.read (4) return read [2] / 100

d function to ga temperatures from MCU (Celsius degree x 100)
‹Ref ga_temp_oray (d):

    # getting ambient tame
    T_a = (iot (d[1540]) + int (d [1541]) • 256) / 100

    # getting raw array of pixels temperie
    raw_data = d [4: 1540]
    T_array =npJrombtdfa(raw_        . ‹type = up.intl6)

    rctura T_a,T_anay

#fiioaiontoconverttemplestopixelsoaimage
def td_to_image(f).
    norm = up.nint8 ((f, 100 - Twin) • 255, (Tmax-Tmin))
    norm.shy = (24.32)
```

————————————————————— Main cycle ======================= =————————
Color map range

```python
Tn       =40
Tmin =20
```

```python
print ('Corifi guring Seri d  port')
ser = seri d .Seri d (' dev ." seri d 0')
ser.baucYate = 115200

= set frequency' of module to 4 Hz
ser.site (seri d.to baies ([0xA5  0x25  0x01  0xCB]))
time.s l eep  (0.1)

= Starting automati c data colecti on
ser.site (seri d.to baies ([0xA5  0x35  0x02  0xD/)
t0 = time.time  Q



while True.
= waiting for data frame
data = ser.read  (1544)

= The data is ready' l et's handle it!
To tanp array' = get temp  array' (data)
ta img = td to image  (temp array')

= Guage processing
img = cv2.appl vColorñlap (ta img cv2.COL ORñfAP JE T)
img = cv2.rest ze (inn g (320 240) interpolati on = cv2.IhMR  GB  IC)
img = cv2 Hi p (inn g l)


text = Tmin = {. +. 1f) Tmax  = {. +. 1f) FPS = {. .2f)'. format (temp
array'.min () ." 100 temp array'.max Q ." 100
1 ." (time .time Q - t0))
cv2.putText (img text (5 15) cv2.FONT HERSHEY SET&LE X 0.45 (0
0 0) 1)
cv2.imshou' ('Output' img)

* if 's' is pressed - savi ng of picture key' = cv2.waitKe\' (1) & 0xFF
if key'    ord (" s").
fname = 'pic ' + dt.datetime.now' Q. strfli me (". o Y-°. o m-°. » d °. » H-°. » ñl-
°. » S) + '.jpg' cv2.imuñte (fnam e img)
print ('Savi rig image' fnam e) t0 = time.time  Q




except KevboardInterrupt.
* to terminate the cycle
ser.site (seri d.to baies ([0xA5  0x35 0x01 0xDB])) ser.close Q
cv2.destrovAl1fi'indows Q print ('Stopped)

= just in case ser.close Q
cv2.destrovAl1fi'indows Q
```

Results

The script polls the thermal imaging matrix and outputs the frames to the monitor console on which the Raspberry PI is connected, four times per second. This is enough not to experience significant discomfort when shooting objects. To visualize the frame, the OpenCV package is used. When the "s" button is pressed, the thermal imaging "heat maps" in jpg format are saved in the folder with the script.

For more information, I deduced the minimum and maximum temperatures on the frame. That is, looking at the color, you can see what approximately the temperature of the most heated or chilled objects. The measurement error is approximately a degree with a larger side. The thermal range is set from 20 to 40 degrees. Exit the script by pressing Ctrl + C.

The script works approximately the same on both the Raspberry Pi Zero W and the Pi 3 B +. I installed the VNC server on the smartphone. Thus, picking up raspberries connected to a power bank and a smartphone with VNC running, you can get a portable thermal imager with the ability to save thermal images. Perhaps this is not entirely convenient, but quite functional. After the first start, an incorrect measurement of the maximum temperature is possible. In this case, you need to exit the script and rerun it.

That is all for today. The experiment with a home-made thermal imager turned out to be successful. With the helping of this device, it is quite possible to conduct a thermal imaging inspection of the house on your own, for example.

Due to the lower temperature contrast than indoors, the pictures were not very informative. In the photo above, the whole house is on two sides. On the bottom - photos of different windows.

In the code, I changed only the temperature range. Instead of +20 ... + 40, I set -10 ... + 5.

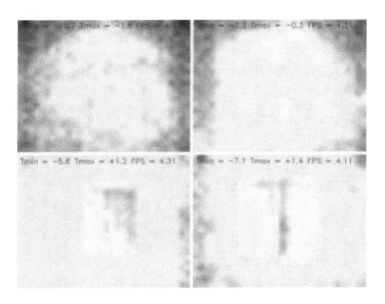

Finding a Free Parking Space with Python

I live in a proper city. But, like in many others, the search for a parking space always turns into a test. Free spaces quickly occupy, and even if you have your own, it will be difficult for friends to call you because they will have nowhere to park.

So I decided to point the camera out the window and use deep learning so that my computer tells me when the space is available:

It may sound complicated, but writing a working prototype with deep learning is quick and easy. All the necessary components are already there - you just need to know where to find them and how to put them together.

So let's have some fun and write an accurate free parking notification system using Python and deep learning

Decomposing the task

When we have a difficult task that we want to solve with the help of machine learning, the first step is to break it down into a sequence of simple tasks. Then we can use various tools to solve each of them. By combining several simple solutions, we get a system that is capable of something complex.

Here is how I broke my task:

The video stream from the webcam directed to the window enters the conveyor input: Through the pipeline, we will transmit each frame of the video, one at a time.

The first point is to recognize all the possible parking spaces in the frame. Before we can look for unoccupied places, we need to understand in which parts of the image there is parking.

Then on each frame you need to find all the cars. This will allow us to track the movement of each machine from frame to frame. The third step is to determine which places are occupied by machines and which are not. To do this, combine the results of the first two steps.

Finally, the program should send an alert when the parking space becomes free. This will be determined by changes in the location of the machines between the frames of the video.

Each of the step can be completed in different ways using different technologies. There is no single right or wrong way to compose this conveyor: different approaches will have their advantages and disadvantages. Let's deal with each step in more detail.

We recognize parking spaces

Here is what our camera sees:

We need to scan this image somehow and get a list of places to park:

The solution "in the forehead" would be to simply hardcode the locations of all parking spaces manually instead of automatically recognizing them. But in this case, if we move the camera or want to look for parking spaces on another street, we will have to do the whole procedure again. It sounds so-so, so let's look for an automatic way to recognize parking spaces.

Alternatively, you can search for parking meters in the image and assume that there is a parking space next to each of them:

However, with this approach, not everything is so smooth.

Firstly, not every parking space has a parking meter, and indeed, we are more interested in finding parking spaces for which you do not have to pay. Secondly, the location of the parking meter does not tell us anything about where the parking space is, but it only allows us to make an assumption.

Another idea is to create an object recognition model that looks for parking space marks drawn on the road:

But this approach is so-so. Firstly, in my city, all such trademarks are very small and difficult to see at a distance, so it will be difficult to detect them using a computer. Secondly, the street is full of all sorts of other lines and marks. It will be challenging to separate parking marks from lane dividers and pedestrian crossings.

When you encounter a problem that at first glance seems complicated, take a few minutes to find another approach to solving the problem, which will help to circumvent some technical issues. What is the parking space? This is just a place where a car is parked for a long time. Perhaps we do not need to recognize parking spaces at all. Why don't we acknowledge only cars that have stood still for a long time and not assume that they are standing in a parking space?

In other words, parking spaces are located where cars stand for a long time:

Thus, if we can recognize the cars and find out which of them do not move between frames, we can guess where the parking spaces are. Simple as that - let's move on to recognizing cars!

Recognize cars

Recognizing cars on a video frame is a classic object recognition task. There are many machine learning approaches that we could use for recognition. Here are some of them in order from the "old school" to the "new school":

You can train the detector based on HOG (Histogram of Oriented Gradients, histograms of directional gradients) and walk it through the entire image to find all the cars. This old approach, which does not use deep learning, works relatively quickly but does not cope very well with machines located in different ways.

You can train a CNN-based detector (Convolutional Neural Network, a convolutional neural network) and walk through the entire image until you find all the cars. This approach works precisely, but not as efficiently since we need to scan the image several times using CNN to find all the machines. And although we can find machines located in different ways, we need much more training data than for a HOG detector.

You can use a new approach with deep learning like Mask R-CNN, Faster R-CNN, or YOLO, which combines the accuracy of CNN and a set of technical tricks that significantly increase the speed of recognition. Such models will work relatively quickly (on the GPU) if we have a lot of data for training the model.

In the general case, we need the simplest solution, which will work as it should and require the least amount of training data. This is not required to be the newest and fastest algorithm. However, specifically in our case, Mask R- CNN is a reasonable choice, even though it is unique and fast.

Mask R-C-N-N architecture is designed in such a way that it recognizes objects in the entire image, effectively spending resources, and does not use the sliding window approach. In other words, it works pretty fast. With a modern GPU, we can recognize objects in the video in high resolution at a speed of several frames per second. For our project, this should be enough.

Also, Mask R-CNN provides a lot of information about each recognized object. Most recognition algorithms return only a bounding box for each object. However, Mask R-CNN will not only give us the location of each object but also its outline (mask):

To train Mask R-CNN, we need a lot of images of the objects that we want to recognize. We could go outside, take pictures of cars, and mark them in photographs, which would require several days of work. Fortunately, cars are one of those objects that people often want to recognize, so several public datasets with images of cars already exist.

One of them is the popular SOCO dataset (short for Common Objects In Context), which has images annotated with object masks. This dataset contains over 12,000 images with already labeled machines. Here is an example image from the dataset: Such data is excellent for training a model based on Mask R-CNN.

But hold the horses, there is news even better! We are not the first who wanted to train their model using the COCO dataset - many people had already done this before us and shared their results. Therefore, instead of training our model, we can take a ready-made one that can already recognize cars. For our project, we will use the open-sourcemodel from Matterport.

If we give the image from the camera to the input of this model, this is what we get already "out of the box":

The model recognized not only cars but also objects such as traffic lights and people. It's funny that she recognized the tree as a houseplant.

For each recognized object, the Mask R-CNN model returns four things:

Type of object detected (integer). The pre-trained COCO model can recognize 80 different everyday objects like cars and trucks. A complete list is available here.

The degree of confidence in the recognition results. The higher the number, the stronger the model is confident in the correct recognition of the object.

Abounding box for an object in the form of XY-coordinates of pixels in the image.

A "mask" that shows which pixels within the bounding box are part of the object. Using the mask data, you can find the outline of the object.

Below is the Python code for detecting the bounding box for machines using the pre-trained Mask R-CNN and OpenCV models:

```
import nump\' as up

import mrcnn config import mrcnn.utils
from mrcnn.model import ñlaskRCNN from pathli b import Path


= The corfi gur ati on that the flask-RCNN librm.' u411 use. class
ñlaskRCNNCorfi g (mrcnn config Colt g.
    DUE  = " coco   retr ained model corifi g" EvfAGES PER GPL = 1
    GPL COLNT   1
    h    I CLASSES = 1 + 80= in the COCO dataset there are 80 classes +
    1 background class. DETECTION  UHN CONFIDENCE = 0.6
```

= fi'e filter the list of r ecogniti on results so that onl\' cars remain. def get car boxes (boxes class i ds).

    car boxes = Q

    for i box in enumerate (boxes).

      = If the found obj eO is not a car them skip it. if class ids [i] in [3 8 6].

        car boxes. append (box) return up. array' (car boxes)

= The root direct∝\' of the project. ROOT DIR = Path (".")

= Dir eO w.' for savi rig logs and trained model. ñlODEL DIR = ROOT DIR .' " logs"

* Locd path to the fi l e with trained weights.
COCO ñlODEL PATH = ROOT DIR .' " mask rem coco.h5"

= Dourload COCO dataset if necessary'. if not COCO ñlODEL PATH. exists Q.
    mrcnn.uti l s.dourload trained weights (COCO ñlODEL PATH)

= Dir eO w.' with images for processing. EvfAGE DIR = ROOT DIR .' "images"

= \'i deo fi l e or camera for processing - insert a vd ue of 0 if you want to use a cam era not a video file. VIDEO SOFF CE " test images .'' parking.m@"

= Create a flask-RCNN model in output mode.
model = ñlaskR WU (mode = '' inference" model dir = ñlODEL DIR corifi g = ñlaskR C UCorifi g Q)

= Dourload the pre-train ed model.
modd. l oad weights (COCO ñlODEL PATH b\' name = True)

* Locati ∝i of parking spaces.
pznked cr boies=hone

```python
# Download the video file for which we want to run recognition.
video_capture = cv2.VideoCapture (VIDEO_SOURCE)

# We loop through each frame.
while video_capture.isOpened ():
    success, frame = video_capture.read ()
    if not success:
        break

    # Convert the image from the BGR color model (used by OpenCV) to RGB.
    rgb_image = frame [:, :, ::-1]

    # We supply the image of the Mask R-CNN model to get the result.
    results = model.detect ([rgb_image], verbose = 0)

    # Mask R-CNN assumes that we recognize objects in multiple images.
    # We transmitted only one image, so we extract only the first result.
    r = results [0]

    # The variable r now contains recognition results:
    # - r ['rois'] - bounding box for each recognized object.
    # - r ['class_ids'] - identifier (type) of the object.
    # - r ['scores'] - degree of confidence.
    # - r ['masks'] - masks of objects (which gives you their outline).

    # Filter the result to get the scope of the car.
    car_boxes = get_car_boxes (r ['rois'], r ['class_ids'])

    print ("Cars found in frame of video:")

    # Display each frame on the frame.
    for box in car_boxes:
        print ("Car", box)

        y1, x1, y2, x2 = box

        # Draw a frame.
        cv2.rectangle (frame, (x1, y1), (x2, y2), (0, 255, 0), 1)

    # Show the frame on the screen.
    cv2.imshow ('Video', frame)

    # Press 'q' to exit.
    if cv2.waitKey (1) & 0xFF == ord ('q'):
        break

# We clear everything after completion.
video_capture.release ()
cv2.destroyAllWindows ()
```

After running this script, an image with a frame around each detected machine will appear on the screen: Also, the coordinates of each machine will be displayed in the console:

Cars found in frame of video:
Car: [492 871 551 961]
Car: [450 819 509 913]
Car: [411 774 470 856]

So we learned to recognize cars in the image.

We recognize empty parking spaces

We know the pixel coordinates of each machine. Looking through several consecutive frames, we can quickly determine which of the cars did not move and assume that there are parking spaces. But how to understand that the car left the parking lot?

The problem is that the frames of the machines partially overlap each other:

Therefore, if you imagine that each frame represents a parking space, it may turn out that it is partially occupied by the machine, when in fact it is empty. We need to find a way to measure the degree of intersection of two objects to search only for the "most empty" frames.

We will use a measure called Intersection Over Union (ratio of intersection area to total area) or IoU. IoU can be found by calculating the number of pixels where two objects intersect and divide by the number of pixels occupied by these objects:

So we can understand how the very bounding frame of the car intersects with the frame of the parking space. make it easy to determine if parking is free. If the IoU is low, like 0.15, then the car takes up a small part of the parking space. And if it is high, like 0.6, then this means that the car takes up most of the space and you can't park there.

Since IoU is used quite often in computer vision, it is very likely that the corresponding libraries implement this measure. In our library Mask R-CNN, it is implemented as a function mrcnn.utils.compute_overlaps ().

If we have a list of bounding boxes for parking spaces, you can add a check for the presence of cars in this framework by adding a whole line or two of code:

```
# Filter the result to get the scope of the car.
car_boxes = get_car_boxes (r ['rois'], r ['class_ids'])

# We look how much cars intersect with well-known parking spaces.
overlaps = mrcnn.utils.compute_overlaps (car_boxes, parking_areas)

print (overlaps)
```

The result should look something like this:

```
[
 [1. 0.07040032 0. 0.]
 [0.07040032 1. 0.07673165 0.]
 [0. 0. 0.023321112 0.]
]
```

In this two-dimensional array, each row reflects one frame of the parking space. And each column indicates how strongly each of the places intersects with one of the detected machines. A result of 1.0 means that the entire space is entirely occupied by the car, and a low value like 0.02 indicates that the car has climbed into place a little, but you can still park on it.

To find unoccupied places, you just need to check each row in this array. If all numbers are close to zero, then most likely, the place is free!

However, keep in mind that object recognition does not always work correctly with real-time video. Although the model based on Mask R-CNN is wholly accurate, from time to time, it may miss a car or two in one frame of the video. Therefore, before asserting that the place is free, you need to make sure that it remains so for the next 5-10 next frames of video. This way, we can avoid situations when the system mistakenly marks a place empty due to a glitch in one frame of the video. As soon as we make sure that the place remains free for several frames, you can send a message!

Send SMS

The last part of our conveyor is sending SMS notifications when a free parking space appears.

Sending a message from Python is very easy if you use Twilio. Twilio is an accessible API that allows you to send SMS from almost any programming language with just a few lines of code.

Of course, if you prefer a different service, you can use it. I have nothing to do with Twilio: it's just the first thing that come to brain .

To using Twilio, sign-up for a trial account, create a Twilio phone number, and get your account authentication information. Then install the client library:

```
pip install twilio
```

After that, use the following code to send the message:

```python
from twilio.rest import Client

# Twilio account details.
twilio_account_sid = 'Your Twilio SID'
twilio_auth_token = 'Your Twilio Authentication Token'
twilio_source_phone_number = 'Your Twilio Phone Number'

# Create a Twilio client object.
client = Client (twilio_account_sid, twilio_auth_token)

# Send SMS.
message = client.messages.create (
    body = 'Message body',
    from_ = twilio_source_phone_number,
    to = 'Your number where the message will come'
)
```

To add the ability to send messages to our script, just copy this code there. However, you need make sure that the message is not sent on every frame, where you can see the free space. Therefore, we will have a flag that in the installed state will not allow sending messages for some time or until another place is vacated.

Putting it all together

```
import numpy as np
import cv2
import mrcnn.config
import mrcnn.utils
```

```python
from mrcnn.model import MaskRCNN
from pathlib import Path
from twilio.rest import Client

# The configuration that the Mask-RCNN library will use.
class MaskRCNNConfig (mrcnn.config.Config):
    NAME = "coco_pretrained_model_config"
    IMAGES_PER_GPU = 1
    GPU_COUNT = 1
    NUM_CLASSES = 1 + 80 # in the COCO dataset there are 80 classes + 1 background class.
    DETECTION_MIN_CONFIDENCE = 0.6

# We filter the list of recognition results so that only cars remain.
def get_car_boxes (boxes, class_ids):
    car_boxes = []

    for i, box in enumerate (boxes):
        # If the found object is not a car, then skip it.
        if class_ids [i] in [3, 8, 6]:
            car_boxes.append (box)

    return np.array (car_boxes)

# Twilio configuration.
twilio_account_sid = 'Your Twilio SID'
twilio_auth_token = 'Your Twilio Authentication Token'
twilio_phone_number = 'Your Twilio Phone Number'
destination_phone_number = 'Number where the message will come'
client = Client (twilio_account_sid, twilio_auth_token)

# The root directory of the project.
ROOT_DIR = Path (".")

# Directory for saving logs and trained model.
MODEL_DIR = ROOT_DIR / "logs"

# Local path to the file with trained weights.
COCO_MODEL_PATH = ROOT_DIR / "mask_rcnn_coco.h5"

# Download COCO dataset if necessary.
if not COCO_MODEL_PATH.exists ():
    mrcnn.utils.download_trained_weights (COCO_MODEL_PATH)

# Directory with images for processing.
IMAGE_DIR = ROOT_DIR / "images"

# Video file or camera for processing - insert the value 0 if using a camera, not a video file.
VIDEO_SOURCE = "test_images / parking.mp4"

# Create a Mask-RCNN model in output mode.
model = MaskRCNN (mode = "inference", model_dir = MODEL_DIR, config = MaskRCNNConfig ())

# Download the pre-trained model.
model.load_weights (COCO_MODEL_PATH, by_name = True)
```

Location of parking spaces.

```
parked_car_boxes= None

    Douml oad the st deo file for vhlch ve vant t D run recDgM ti or.
video_capture = eve.\'ideoCapture /fiDE O_S OURCE)

.=. How' mans' frames in a row' math an mnpR.' place we have already' seen.
free space frames = 0

.=. Have w'e d ready sent SMS?
sms sent = Fd se

  "e l cop thfDugh each frame.
whil e s4 deD Capture.isOpened 0
    success, frame = video_capture.read ()
    if not success:
        break

    Corivert the image from the BGR col or model to RGB .
    rgb_ mage = frame [.... .: − I]

    # fi'e supply' the image of the flask R—Ch   model to get the result.
    results = mDdel.detect ([r gb image], s erbDse = 0)

    flask R-CA assumes that 'e recognize  objects in multiple images.
= fi'e tr aris iitted onl>' one imag e, sD we extract OflI\' the fir st result.
    r = results [0]

= The variable r now' contains recogniti on results.
    = - r rois'] - bounding box for each recognized object:
    - r class ids'] - identifier (type) of the object:
    - r § scar est - degree D f cDn 1 dence:
= -r  masks    masks of objects ( 'hich gi yes von their outline).

    if parked car boxes i s None:
        = Thi s is the first frame Df the videD - let's say' that all detected cars are in the parking l ot.
        = Save the locad on of each car as a parking space and move on tD the next fratne.
        parked_car_boxes = get_car_boxes (• L•ois'], r cl ass_i ds'])
    else:
        = XVe dread>' knor' where the places are. Check if there are an>'.

        = U'e ar e l DDki fly for KOf.S Dn the oirr cut fram e.
        car_boxes = get_car_boxes (r ['r∝ sd . L+         '])

            l'e 1Dok hDT' rauch these cars I ntersect a'tth 'ell -knDTW parking
        DS'erl aps = rarcnn.uti ls.co tpute_a'er1 aps {parked_car_bDxes, car_boxes)

        = XVe assume that there are no emph.' seats until 'e find at l east one.
        free_space = Fal se

        = XVe go through the cycle for each well-known parking space.
        fa parking_area. overl ap_areas in zip (parked_car_boxes. overl aps):
```

= fi'e are lDDkiflg for the maximum seal ue of the intersectiDH Flth an›' detected
Dn the frame b5' the machine (no matter w'hich).
max_I oU_overl ap = up.max (overlap_areas)

```
# We get the upper left and lower right coordinates of the parking space
    y1, x1, y2, x2 = parking_area

    # Check if space is free by checking the IoU value.
    if max_IoU_overlap <0.15:
        # Place is free! Draw a green frame around it
        cv2.rectangle (frame, (x1, y1), (x2, y2), (0, 255, 0), 3)
        # We note that we found at least it is free space
        free_space = True
    else:
        # The place is still taken - we draw a red frame
        cv2.rectangle (frame, (x1, y1), (x2, y2), (0, 0, 255), 1)

        # Write the IoU value inside the frame.
        font = cv2.FONT_HERSHEY_DUPLEX
        cv2.putText (frame, f ' {max_IoU_overlap: 0.2}", (x1 + 6, y2 - 6), font, 0.3, (255, 255, 255))

    # If at least one place was free, we begin to count frames
    # This is to make sure that the place is really free
    # and do not send another notification.
    if free_space:
        free_space_frames += 1
    else:
        # If everything is busy, reset the counter
        free_space_frames = 0

    # If the place is free for several frames, we can say that it is free.
    if free_space_frames> 10:
        # Display SPACE AVAILABLE !! at the top of the screen.
        font = cv2.FONT_HERSHEY_DUPLEX
        cv2.putText (frame, f 'SPACE AVAILABLE!", (10, 150), font, 3 0, (0, 255, 0), 2, cv2.FILLED)

        # Send a message if you have not done so already.
        if not sms_sent:
            print ("SENDING SMS !!!")
            message = client.messages.create (
                body = "Parking space open - go go go!",
                from_ = twilio_phone_number,
                to = destination_phone_number
            )
            sms_sent = True

    # Show the frame on the screen.
    cv2.imshow ('Video', frame)

# Press 'q' to exit.
if cv2.waitKey (1) & 0xFF == ord ('q')
    break

# Press 'q' to exit.
video_capture.release ()
cv2.destroyAllWindows ()
```

To run that code, you first need to install Python 3.6+, Matterport Mask R-CNN, and OpenCV.

I specifically wrote the code as simple as possible. For example, if he sees in the first frame of the car, he concludes that they are all parked. Try experiment with it and see if you can improve its reliability.

Just by changing the identifiers of the objects that the model is looking for, you can turn the code into something completely different. For example, imagine that you are working at a ski resort. After making a couple of changes, you can turn this script into a system that automatically recognizes snowboarders jumping from a ramp and records videos with cool jumps. Or, if you work in a nature reserve, you can create a system that counts zebras. You are limited only by your imagination.

Creating games on the Pygame framework | Part 1

Hi, Python lover!

This is the first of a third-part tutorial on creating games using Python 3 and Pygame. In the second part, we examined the class TextObjectused to render text to the screen is created to the main window, and learned how to draw objects: bricks, ball, and racket.

In this part, we will the dive deeper into the heart of Breakout, and learn how to handle events, get acquainted with the main Breakout class, and see how to move various objects in the game.

Event handling

Breakout has three types of events: keystroke events, mouse events, and timer events. The main loop in the Game class handles keystrokes and mouse events and passes them to subscribers (by calling a handler function).

Although the Game class is very general and does not have knowledge about Breakout implementation, the subscription and event handling methods are very specific.

Breakout class

The Breakout class implements most of the knowledge about how Breakout is controlled. In this tutorial series, we will meet the Breakout class several times. Here are the lines that various event handlers register.

It should be noted that all key events (for both the left and right "arrows") are transmitted to one racket handler method.

```
# Register the handle_mouse_event () method of the button object
self.mouse_handlers.append (b.handle_mouse_event)

# Register racket handle () method for handling key events
self.keydown_handlers [pygame.K_LEFT] .append (paddle.handle)
self.keydown_handlers [pygame.K_RIGHT] .append (paddle.handle)
self.keyup_handlers [pygame.K_LEFT] .append (paddle.handle)
self.keyup_handlers [pygame.K_RIGHT] .append (paddle.handle)
```

Keystroke handling

The Game class calls registered handlers for each key event and passes the key. Note that this is not a Paddle

class. Into Breakout, the only object that is interested in such events is a racket. When you press or release a key, its method is handle()called. The Paddle object does not need to know if this was a key press or release event, because it controls the current state using a pair of Boolean variables: moving_left and moving_right. If moving_left True, it means that the "left" key was pressed, and the next event will be the release of the key, which will reset the variable. The same applies to the right key. The logic is simple and consists of switching the state of these variables in response to any event.

```
def handle (self, key):
    if key == pygame.K_LEFT:
        self.moving_left = not self.moving_left
    else:
        self.moving_right = not self.moving_right
```

Mouse event handling

Breakout has a game menu that we will meet soon. The menu
button controls various mouse events, such as movement and
button presses (mouse down and mouse up events). In the
response to these events, the button updates the internal state
variable. Here is the mouse processing code:

```
def handle_mouse_event (self, type, pos):
    if type == pygame.MOUSEMOTION:
        self.handle_mouse_move (pos)
    elif type == pygame.MOUSEBUTTONDOWN:
        self.handle_mouse_down (pos)
    elif type == pygame.MOUSEBUTTONUP:
        self.handle_mouse_up (pos)

def handle_mouse_move (self, pos):
    if self.bounds.collidepoint (pos):
        if self.state != 'pressed':
            self.state = 'hover'
    else:
        self.state = 'normal'

def handle_mouse_down (self, pos):
    if self.bounds.collidepoint (pos):
        self.state = 'pressed'

def handle_mouse_up (self, pos):
    if self.state == 'pressed':
        self.on_click (self)
        self.state = 'hover'
```

Notice that the method handle_mouse_event() registered to receive mouse events checks the type of event and redirects it to the appropriate method that processes this type of event.

Handling Timer Events

Timer events are not processed in the main loop. However, since the main loop is called in each frame, it is easy to check whether the time has come for a particular event. You will see this later when we discuss temporary special effects.

Another situation is the need to pause the game. For example, when displaying a message that the player must read and so that nothing distracts him. The show_message()Breakout class method takes this approach and to calls time.sleep(). Here is the relevant code:

```
import config as c

class Breakout (Game):
    def show_message (self,
            text
            color = colors.WHITE,
            font_name = 'Arial',
            font_size = 20,
            centralized = False):
        message = TextObject (c.screen_width // 2,
                c.screen_height // 2,
                lambda: text, color,
                font_name, font_size)
        self.draw ()
        message.draw (self.surface, centralized)
        pygame.display.update ()
        time.sleep (c.message_duration)
```

Game process

Gameplay (gameplay) is where the Breakout rules come into play. The gameplay consists in moving various objects in response to events and in changing the state of the game based on their interactions.

Moving racket

You saw earlier that the Paddle class responds to arrow keys by updating its
fields *moving_left* and *moving_right*. The movement itself occurs in a method *update()*. Certain calculations are performed here if the racket is close to the left or right edge of the screen. We do not want the racket to go beyond the boundaries of the screen (taking into account a given offset).

Therefore, if the movement moves the object beyond the borders, then the code adjusts the movement so that it stops right at the border. Since the racket only moves horizontally to the vertical component of the movement is always zero.

```python
import pygame

import config as c
from game_object import GameObject

class Paddle (GameObject):
    def __init__(self, x, y, w, h, color, offset):
        GameObject.__init__(self, x, y, w, h)
        self.color = color
        self.offset = offset
        self.moving_left = False
        self.moving_right = False

    ...

    def update(self):
        if self.moving_left:
            dx = -(min(self.offset, self.left))
        elif self.moving_right:
            dx = min(self.offset, c.screen_width - self.right)
        else:
            return

        self.move(dx, 0)
```

Moving ball

The ball simply uses the functionality of the base class
GameObject, which moves objects based on their speed (its
horizontal and vertical components). As we will soon see, the
speed of a ball is determined by many factors in the Breakout
class. Since the movement consists simply of adding speed to the
current position, the direction in which the ball moves is
completely determined by the speed along the horizontal and
vertical axes.

Setting the initial speed of the ball

The Breakout ball comes out of nowhere at the very beginning of
the game every time a player loses his life. It simply materializes

from the ether and begins to fall either exactly down or at a slight angle. When the ball is created in the method create_ball(), it gets the speed with a random horizontal component in the range from - 2 to 2 and the vertical component specified in the config.py module (the default value is 3).

```
def create_ball (self):
    speed = (random.randint (-2, 2), c.ball_speed)
    self.ball = Ball (c.screen_width // 2,
                c.screen_height // 2,
                c.ball_radius,
                c.ball_color,
                speed)
    self.objects.append (self.ball)
```

Summarize

In this part, we looked at handling events such as keystrokes, mouse movements, and mouse clicks. We also examined some elements of Breakout gameplay: moving the racket, moving the ball, and controlling the speed of the ball.

In the fourth part, we will consider the important topic of collision recognition and see what happens when the ball hits different game objects: a racket, bricks, walls, ceiling, and floor. Then we will pay attention to the game menu. We will create our buttons, which we use as a menu, and will be able to show and hide if necessary.

Creating games on the Pygame framework | Part 2

This is the Second of a Thired-part tutorial on the creating games using Python 3 and Pygame. In the third part, we delved to the heart of Breakout, and learned how to handle events, got acquainted within the main Breakout class and saw how to move different game objects.

In this part, we will learn the how to recognize collisions and what happens to when a ball hits different object: a racket, bricks, walls, ceiling, and floor. Finally, we will look at the important topic of the user interface, and in particular, how to create the menu from your buttons.

Collision Recognition

In games, the objects collide with each other, and Breakout is no exception. The ball is collides with objects. The main method handle_ball_collisions()has a built-in function is called intersect()that is used to the check whether the ball hit the object and where it collided with the object. It returns 'left,' 'right,' 'top,' 'bottom,' or None if the ball does not collide with an object.

```python
def handle_ball_collisions (self):
    def intersect (obj, ball):
        edges = dict (
            left = Rect (obj.left, obj.top, 1, obj.height),
            right = Rect (obj.right, obj.top, 1, obj.height),
            top = Rect (obj.left, obj.top, obj.width, 1),
            bottom = Rect (obj.left, obj.bottom, obj.width, 1))
        collisions = set (edge for edge, rect in edges.items () if
                ball.bounds.colliderect (rect))
        if not collisions:
            return none

        if len (collisions) == 1:
            return list (collisions) [0]

        if 'top' in collisions:
            if ball.centery> = obj.top:
                return 'top'
            if ball.centerx <obj.left:
                return 'left'
            else:
                return 'right'

        if 'bottom' in collisions:
            if ball.centery> = obj.bottom:
                return 'bottom'
            if ball.centerx <obj.left:
                return 'left'
            else:
                return 'right'
```

Collision of a ball with a racket.

When the ball hit the racket, it bounces. If it hit the top of the
racket, it bounces back up, but retains same components
horizontal fast speed.

But if he hit the side of the racket, it bounces to the opposite
side (right or left) and continues to move down until it hits the
floor. The code uses a function intersect().

```
# Kick on the racket
s = self.ball.speed
edge = intersect (self.paddle, self.ball)
if edge is not None:
    self.sound_effects ['paddle_hit']. play ()
if edge == 'top':
 speed_x = s [0]
 speed_y = -s [1]
 if self.paddle.moving_left:
  speed_x -= 1
 elif self.paddle.moving_left:
  speed_x += 1
 self.ball.speed = speed_x, speed_y
elif edge in ('left', 'right'):
 self.ball.speed = (-s [0], s [1])
```

Collision with the floor.

The ball hits to the racket from the side, the ball continues fall and then hits the floor. At this moment, the player to loses his life and the ball is recreated so that game can continue. The game ends when player runs out of life.

```
# Hit the floor
if self.ball.top> c.screen_height:
    self.lives -= 1
 if self.lives == 0:
  self.game_over = True
 else:
  self.create_ball ()
```

Collision with ceiling and walls

When a ball hits the wall or ceiling, it simply bounces off them.

```
# Hit the ceiling
if self.ball.top <0:
    self.ball.speed = (s [0], -s [1])

# Kick against the wall
if self.ball.left <0 or self.ball.right> c.screen_width:
 self.ball.speed = (-s [0], s [1])
```

Collision with bricks

When ball hits a brick, this is the main event the Breakout game - the brick disappeared, the player receives a point, the ball bounce back, and several more events occur (sound effect, and sometimes a special effect), which we will consider later.

To determine that the ball has hit a brick, the code will check if any of the bricks intersects with the ball:

```
#Bump on a brick
for brick in self.bricks:
    edge = intersect (brick, self.ball)
    if not edge:
     continue

    self.bricks.remove (brick)
    self.objects.remove (brick)
    self.score + = self.points_per_brick

    if edge in ('top', 'bottom'):
     self.ball.speed = (s [0], -s [1])
    else:
     self.ball.speed = (-s [0], s [1])
```

Game Menu Design Program

Most games have some kind of U.I. Breakout has simple menu with two buttons, 'PLAY' and 'QUIT.' The menu is display at the beginning of the game and disappears when the player clicks on 'PLAY.'

Let's see how the button and menu are implemented, as well as how they integrate into the game.

Button Creation

Pygame has no built-in UI library. The third-party extensions, but for the menu, we decided to create our buttons. that has three states: normal, highlighted, and press. The normal state when the mouse is not above the buttons, and the highlight state is when the mouse is above the button, the left mouse button not yet press. The press state is when the mouse is above the button, and the player pressed the left mouse button.

The buttons implement as a rectangle with a back ground color and text display on top of it. The button also receive the (onclick function), which is called when the button is clicked.

```
import pygame

from game_object import GameObject
from text_object import TextObject
import config as c


class Button (GameObject):
    def __init__ (self,
            x
            y
            w
            h
            text
            on_click = lambda x: None,
            padding = 0):
        super ().__init__ (x, y, w, h)
        self.state = 'normal'
        self.on_click = on_click

        self.text = TextObject (x + padding,
                    y + padding, lambda: text,
                    c.button_text_color,
                    c.font_name,
                    c.font_size)

    def draw (self, surface):
        pygame.draw.rect (surface,
                self.back_color,
                self.bounds)
        self.text.draw (surface)
```

The button process its own mouse events and changes its internal state based on these events. When the button is in the press state and receives the event *MOUSE BUTTONUP*, this means that the player has press the button and the function is called *on _ click()*.

```
def handle_mouse_event (self, type, pos):
    if type == pygame.MOUSEMOTION:
    self.handle_mouse_move (pos)
    elif type == pygame.MOUSEBUTTONDOWN:
    self.handle_mouse_down (pos)
    elif type == pygame.MOUSEBUTTONUP:
    self.handle_mouse_up (pos)

def handle_mouse_move (self, pos):
    if self.bounds.collidepoint (pos):
    if self.state! = 'pressed':
    self.state = 'hover'
    else:
    self.state = 'normal'

def handle_mouse_down (self, pos):
    if self.bounds.collidepoint (pos):
    self.state = 'pressed'

def handle_mouse_up (self, pos):
    if self.state == 'pressed':
    self.on_click (self)
    self.state = 'hover'
```

The property *back _ color* used to draw on the background rectangle to always returns the color corresponding to current form of the button, so that it is clear to the player that the button is active:

```
@property
def back_color (self):
    return dict (normal = c.button_normal_back_color,
        hover = c.button_hover_back_color,
        pressed = c.button_pressed_back_color) [self.state]
```

Menu Design

The function *create_menu* ()create a menu with two buttons with the text 'PLAY' and 'QUIT.' It has two built- in function, *on _*

play ()and *on _ quit* ()which it pass to the correspond button.
Each button is add to the list *objects* (for rendering), as well as in
the field *menu _ buttons.*

```
def create_menu (self):
    for i, (text, handler) in enumerate (((('PLAY', on_play),
                            ('QUIT, on_quit))):
        b = Button (c.menu_offset_x,
                    c.menu_offset_y + (c.menu_button_h + 5) * i,
                    c.menu_button_w,
                    c.menu_button_h,
                    text
                    handler
                    padding = 5)
        self.objects.append (b)
        self.menu_buttons.append (b)
        self.mouse_handlers.append (b.handle_mouse_event)
```

When PLAY the button is prese *onplay()*, a function is called that
removes the button from the list *object* so that the no longer
drawn. In adding, the values of the Boolean field that trigger the
starting of the game - *is_gamerunningand startlevel-* Thats OK
When the button is press, QUIT is _ game_ runningtakes on
value (False)(in fact, pausing the game), it set game_ over to
True, which triggers the sequence of completion of the game.

```
def on_play (button):
    for b in self.menu_buttons
        self.objects.remove (b)

    self.is_game_running = True
    self.start_level = True

def on_quit (button):
    self.game_over = True
    self.is_game_running = False
```

Show and hide GameMenu

The display and hiding the menu are performed implicitly. When the buttons are in the list object, the menu is visible : when they removed, it is hidden. Everything is very simple.

Create built-in menu with its surface that renders its subcomponents (buttons and other objects) and then simply add or remove these menu components, but this is not required for such a simple menu.

To summarize

We examined the collision recognition and what happens when the ball collides with the different objects: a racket, bricks, walls, floor, and ceiling. We also created a menu with our buttons, which can be hidden and displayed on command.

In last part of the series, we will consider completion of the game, tracking points, and lives, sound effects, and music. We develop complex system of special effects that add few spices to game. Finally, we will the discuss further development and possible improvements.

Creating games on the Pygame framework| Part 3

This is the last of the Thired parts of the tutorial on creating games using Python 3 and PyGame. In the fourth part, we learned to recognize collisions, respond to the fact that the ball collides with different game objects, and created a game menu with its buttons.

In last part, we will look at various topics: the end of the game, managing lives and points, sound effects, music, and even a flexible system of special effects. For dessert, we will consider possible improvements and directions for further development.

End of the game

Sooner or later, the game should end. In this form of Breakout, the game ends in one of two ways: the player either loses all his life or destroys all the bricks. There is no next level in the game (but it can easily be added).

Game over!

The game_overclass of the Game class is set to False in the method init ()of the Game class. The main loop continues until the variable game_overchanges to True :

```
class Game:
    def __init__(self,
            caption
            width
            height
            back_image_filename,
            frame_rate):

        self.game_over = False
        ...

def run(self):
    while not self.game_over:
        self.surface.blit(self.background_image, (0, 0))

        self.handle_events()
        self.update()
        self.draw()

        pygame.display.update()
        self.clock.tick(self.frame_rate)
```

All this happens in the Breakout class in the following cases:

The player presses the QUIT button in the menu.

The player loses his last life.

The player destroys all bricks.

```
def on_quit(button):
    self.game_over = True
    self.is_game_running = False

def handle_ball_collisions(self):

    # Hit the floor
    if self.ball.top > c.screen_height:
        self.lives -= 1
        if self.lives == 0:
            self.game_over = True

            if not self.bricks:
                self.show_message('YOU WIN !!!', centralized = True)
                self.is_game_running = False
                self.game_over = True
                return

def update(self):

    if not self.bricks:
        self.show_message('YOU WIN !!!', centralized = True)
        self.is_game_running = False
        self.game_over = True
        return
```

Game End Message Display

Usually, at the end of the game, we do not want the game window to disappear silently. An exception is a case when we click on the QUIT button in the menu. When a player loses their last life, Breakout displays the traditional message 'GAME OVER!', And when the player wins, it shows the message 'YOU WIN!'

In both cases, the function is used show_message(). It displays text on top of the current screen (the game pauses) and waits a few seconds to before returning. The next iteration of the game loop, checking the field game_overwill determine that it is True, after which the program will end.

This is what the function looks like show_message():

```
def show_message (self,
        text,
        color = colors.WHITE,
        font_name = 'Arial',
        font_size = 20,
        centralized = False):
    message = TextObject (c.screen_width // 2,
            c.screen_height // 2,
            lambda: text,
            color,
            font_name,
            font_size)
    self.draw ()
    message.draw (self.surface, centralized)
    pygame.display.update ()
    time.sleep (c.message_duration)
```

Saving records between games

In this version of the game, we do not save records, because there is only one level in it, and the results of all players after the destruction of the bricks will be the same. In general, saving records can be implemented locally, saving records to a file and displaying another message if a player breaks a record.

Adding Sound Effects and Music

Games are an audiovisual process. Many games have sound effects - short audio clips that are played when a player kills monsters finds a treasure, or a terrible death. Some games also have background music that contributes to the atmosphere. There are only sound effects in Breakout, but we will show you how to play music in your games.

Sound effects

To play sound effects, we need sound files (as is the case with image files). These files can be.wav, .mp3, or .ogg format. Breakout stores its sound effects in a folder sound_effects:

```
~/ git / pygame-breakout> tree sound_effects /
sound_effects /
+- - brick_hit.wav
+- - effect_done.wav
+- - level_complete.wav
+- - paddle_hit.wav
```

Let's see how these sound effects load and play at the right time. First, play sound effects (or background music), we need to initialize the Pygame sound system. This is done in the Game class:pygame.mixer.pre_init(44100, 16, 2, 4096)

Then, in the Breakout class, all sound effects are loaded from config into the object pygame mixer Soundand stored in the dictionary:

```
# In config.py
sounds_effects = dict (
    brick_hit = 'sound_effects / brick_hit.wav',
    effect_done = 'sound_effects / effect_done.wav',
    paddle_hit = 'sound_effects / paddle_hit.wav',
    level_complete = 'sound_effects / level_complete.wav',
)

# In breakout.py
class Breakout (Game):
    def __init__(self):
        ...
        self.sound_effects = {
            name: pygame.mixer.Sound (sound)
            for name, sound in c.sounds_effects.items ()}
        ...
```

Now we can play sound effects when something interesting happens. For example, when a ball hits a brick:

```
#Bump on a brick
for brick in self.bricks:
    edge = intersect (brick, self.ball)
    if not edge:
        continue

    self.sound_effects ['brick_hit']. play ()
```

The sound effect is played asynchronously: that is, the game does not stop while it is playing. Several sound effects can be played at the same time.

Record your sound effects and messages

Recording your sound effects can be a simple and fun experience. Unlike creating visual resources, it does not require much talent. Anyone can say "Boom!" or "Jump," or shout, "They killed you. Get lucky another time! "

Playing background music

Background music should play continuously. Theoretically, a very long sound effect can be created, but the looped background music is most often used. Music files can be in .wav, .mp3, or .midi format. Here's how the music is implemented:

```
music = pygame.mixer.music.load ('background_music.mp3')
pygame.mixer.music.play (-1, 0.0)
```

Only one background music can play at a time. However, several sound effects can be played on top of background music. This is what is called mixing.

Adding Advanced Features

Let's do something curious. It is interesting to destroy bricks with a ball, but it quickly bothers. What about the overall special effects system? We will develop an extensible special effects system associated with some bricks, which is activated when the ball hits the brick.

This is what the plan will be. Effects have a lifetime. The effect begins when the brick collapses and ends when the effect expires. What happens if the ball hits another brick with a special effect? In theory, you can create compatible effects, but to simplify everything in the original implementation, the active effect will stop, and a new effect will take its place.,

Special effects system

In the most general case, a special effect can be defined as two purposes. The first role activates the effect, and the second reset it. We want attach effects to bricks and give the player a clear understanding of which bricks special , so they can try to hit them or avoid them at certain points.

Our special effects are determined by the dictionary from the module breakout.py. Each effect has a name (for example, long_paddle) and a value that consists of a brick color, as well as two functions. Functions are defined a lambda functions that take a Game instance, which includes everything that can change the special effect in Breakout.

```
special_effects = dict (
    long_paddle = (
        colors.ORANGE,
        lambda g: g.paddle.bounds.inflate_ip (
            c.paddle_width // 2, 0),
        lambda g: g.paddle.bounds.inflate_ip (
            -c.paddle_width // 2, 0)),
    slow_ball = (
        colors.AQUAMARINE2,
        lambda g: g.change_ball_speed (-1),
        lambda g: g.change_ball_speed (1)),
    tripple_points = (
        colors.DARKSEAGREEN4,
        lambda g: g.set_points_per_brick (3),
        lambda g: g.set_points_per_brick (1)),
    extra_life = (
        colors.GOLD1,
        lambda g: g.add_life (),
        lambda g: None))
```

When creating bricks, they can be assigned one of the special effects. Here is the code:

```
def create_bricks (self):
    w = c.brick_width
    h = c.brick_height
    brick_count = c.screen_width // (w + 1)
    offset_x = (c.screen_width - brick_count * (w + 1)) // 2

    bricks = []
    for row in range (c.row_count):
        for col in range (brick_count):
            effect = None
            brick_color = c.brick_color
            index = random.randint (0, 10)
            if index < len (special_effects):
                x = list (special_effects.values ()) [index]
                brick_color = x [0]
                effect = x [1:]

            brick = Brick (offset_x + col * (w + 1),
                c.offset_y + row * (h + 1),
                w
                h
                brick_color,
                effect)
            bricks.append (brick)
            self.objects.append (brick)
    self.bricks = bricks
```
The Brick class has an

effect field, which usually has the value None, but (with a probability of 30%) may contain one of the special effects defined above. Note that this code does not know what effects exist. He simply receives the effect and color of the brick and, if necessary, assigns them.

In this version of Breakout, we only trigger effects when we hit a brick, but you can come up with other options for triggering events. The previous effect is discarded (if it existed), and then a new effect is launched. The reset function and effect start time are stored for future use.

```
if brick.special_effect is not None:
    # Reset the previous effect, if any
    if self.reset_effect is not None:
        self.reset_effect (self)

    # Triggering a special effect
    self.effect_start_time = datetime.now ()
    brick.special_effect [0] (self)
    # Setting the current effect reset function
    self.reset_effect = brick.special_effect [1]
```

If the new effect is not launched, we still need to reset the current effect after its lifetime. This happens in the method update(). In each frame, a function to reset the current effect is assigned to the field reset_effect. If the time after starting the current effect exceeds the duration of the effect, then the function is called reset_effect(), and the field reset_effecttakes the value None (meaning that there are currently no active effects).

```
# Reset special effect if necessary
if self.reset_effect:
    elapsed = datetime.now () - self.effect_start_time
    if elapsed >= timedelta (seconds = c.effect_duration):
        self.reset_effect (self)
        self.reset_effect = None
```

Racket increase

The effect of a long racket is to increase the racket by 50%. Its reset function returns the racket to its normal size. The brick has the color Orange.:

```
long_paddle = (
    colors.ORANGE,
    lambda g: g.paddle.bounds.inflate_ip (
        c.paddle_width // 2, 0),
    lambda g: g.paddle.bounds.inflate_ip (
        -c.paddle_width // 2, 0)),
```

Ball slowdown

Another effect that helps in chasing the ball is slowing the ball, that is, reducing its speed by one unit. The brick has an Aquamarine color.

```
slow_ball = (colors.AQUAMARINE2,
    lambda g: g.change_ball_speed (-1),
    lambda g: g.change_ball_speed (1)),
```

More points

If you want great results, then you will like the effect of tripling points, giving three points for each destroyed brick instead of the standard one point. The brick is dark green.

```
tripple_points = (colors.DARKSEAGREEN4,
        lambda g: g.set_points_per_brick (3),
        lambda g: g.set_points_per_brick (1)),
```

Extra lives

Finally, a very useful effect will be the effect of extra lives. He just gives you another life. It does not need a reset. The brick has a gold color.

```
extra_life = (colors.GOLD1,
        lambda g: g.add_life (),
        lambda g: None))
```

Future Features

There are several logical directions for expanding Breakout. If you are interested in trying on yourself in adding new features and functions, here are a few ideas.

Go to the next level

To turn Breakout into a serious game, you need levels: one is not enough. At the beginning of each level, we will reset the screen, but save points and lives. To complicate the game, you can slightly increase the speed of the ball at each level or add another layer of bricks.

Second ball

The effect of temporarily adding a second ball will create enormous chaos. The difficulty here is to treat both balls as equal, regardless of which one is the original. When one ball disappears, the game continues with the only remaining. Life is not lost.

Lasting records

When you have levels with increasing difficulty, it is advisable to create a high score table. You can store records in a file so that they are saved after the game. When a player breaks a record, you can add small pizzas or let him write a name (traditionally with only three characters).

Bombs and bonuses

In the current implementation on, all special effects are associated with bricks, but you can add effects (good and bad) falling from the sky, which the player can collect or avoid.

Summarize

Developing Breakout with Python 3 and Pygame has proven to be an enjoyable experience. This is a compelling combination for creating 2D games (and for 3D games too). If you love Python and want to create your games, then do not hesitate to choose Pygame.

Object-Oriented Programming (OOP) in Python 3

Algorithms and data structures

Hi, Python lover!

Table of contents

What is object-oriented programming (OOP)?

Python classes

Python Object (Instances)

How to define class in Python Instance Attribute Class Attributes

Object CreationWhat's it? Exercise Overview (# 1)

Instance MethodsChanging Attributes

Python object inheritance Example of a dog park Expansion of
parent class functionality Parent and child classes Overriding
parent class functionality Exercise overview (# 2)

Conclusion

you will become familiars with the following basic concepts of
OOP in Python:

Python Classes

Object Instances

Definition and work with methods

OOP Inheritance

What is object-oriented programming (OOP)?

Object-oriented programming, or, in short, OOP, is a programming paradigm that provides a means of structuring programs in such a way that properties and behavior are combined into separate objects.

For example, an object can represent a person with a name, age, address, etc., with behaviors such as walking, talking, breathing, and running. Or an email with properties such as a recipient list, subject, body, etc., as well as with behaviors such as adding attachments and sending.

In other words, object-oriented programming is an approach for modeling specific real things, such as cars, as well as the relationships between things like companies and employees, students and teachers, etc. OOP models real objects as program objects that have some data that are associated with it and can performs certain function.

Another common program para-digm is procedural program, which structure a program like a recipe in the sense that it provides a set of steps in the form of functions and blocks of code that are executed sequentially to complete a task.

The key conclusion is that objects are at the center of the paradigm of object-oriented programming, representing not only data, as in procedural programming, but also in the general structure of the program.

NOTE Since Python is a programming language with many paradigms, you can choose the paradigm that is best suited to the problem in question, mix different para-digms in one program or switching from one para-digm to another as your program develops.

Python classes

Focusing first on the data, each object or thing is an instance of some class.

The primitive data structures available in Python, such as numbers, strings, and lists, are designed to represent simple things, such as the value of something, the name of the poem, and your favorite colors, respectively.

What if you want to imagine something much more complex? For example, let say you wanted to track several different animals. If you use a list, the first element may be the name of the animal, while the second element may represent its age. How would you know which element should be? What if you had 100 different animals? Are you sure that every animal has a name, age, and so on? What if you want to add other properties to these animals? This is not enough organization, and this is exactly what you need for classes.

Classes are used to create new user data structure that contain arbitrary informations abouts some thing. In this case of an animal, we could creates an Animal()class to track animal properties such as name and age.

It is importants to note that a class simply provides structure - it is an example of how something should be defined, but in fact, it does not provide any real content. Animal()The class may indicate that the name and age are required to determine the animal, but it will not claim that the name or age of a particular animal is.

This can help present the class as an idea of how something should be defined.

Python Objects (Instances)

While a class is a plan, an instance is a copy of a class with actual values, literally an object belonging to a particular class. This is no longer an idea: it's a real animal, like a dog named Roger, which is eight years old.

In other words, a class is a form or profile. It determines the necessary informations. After you fullfill out the form, your

specific copy is an instance of the class: it contains up-to-date
information relevant to you.

You can fill out several copies to create many different copies,
but without a form, as a guide, you would be lost without
knowing what information is required. Thus, before you can
create separate instances of an object, we must first specify
what you need by defining a class.

How to define a class in Python

Defining a class is simple in Python:

```
class Dog:
    pass
```

You start with a classkeyword to indicate that you are creating a
class, then you add the class name (using theCamelCase notation
starting with a capital letter).

Also here we used the Python keyword pass. This is huge often
used as a placeholder where the code will eventually go. This
allows us to run this code without generating an error.

Note: the above code is correct in Python 3. On Python 2.x
("deprecated Python"), you would use a slightly different class
definition:

```
# Python 2.x Class Definition
class Dog (object):
    pass
```

Not the (object)parts in parentheses indicate the parent class that you are inheriting from (more on this below). In Python-3, this is no longer necessary because it is implicit by defaulting.

Instance attribute

All class create objects, and all objects contain characteristics called attributes (called properties in the first paragraph). Use the init ()method to initialize (for example, determine) the initial attributes of an object by giving them a default value (state). This method must have atleast one argument, as well as a self variable that refers to the object itself (for example, Dog).

```
class Dog

# Initializer / Instance Attributes
def __init__(self name, age):
    self.name = name
    self.age = age
```

In our Dog()class, each dog has a specific name and age, which is certainly important to know when you start creating different dogs. Remember: the class is intended only to define a dog, and not to create instances of individual dogs with specific names and ages: we will come back to this soon.

Similarly, a self variable is also an instance of a class. Since class instances have different meanings, we could argue, Dog.name = namenot self.name = name. But since not all dogs have the same name, we must be able to assign different values for different instances. Hence the need for a special self variable that will help track individual instances of each class.

NOTE: you will never have to call a init ()method: it is called automatically when a new instance of Dog is created.

Class attributes

Although instance attributes are specific to each object, class attributes are the same for all instances, in this case, all dogs.

```
class Dog:

    # Class Attribute
    species = 'mammal'

    # Initializer / Instance Attributes
    def __init__(self, name, age):
        self.name = name
        self.age = age
```

Thus, although each dog has a unique name and age, each dog will be a mammal. Let's create some dogs ...

Create Objects

Instantiating is an unusual term for creating a new unique instance of a class.

For example: >>>

```
>>> class Dog:
... pass
...
>>> Dog ()
<__main__.Dog object at 0x1004ccc50>
>>> Dog ()
<__main__.Dog object at 0x1004ccc90>
>>> a = Dog ()
>>> b = Dog ()
>>> a == b
False
```

We started by define a new Dog()class, then created two new

dogs, each of which was assigned to different

objects. So, to create an instance of the class, you use the class

name follow by parentheses. Then, to demonstration that each

instance is actually different, we created two more dogs,

assigning each variable, and then checking to see if these

variables are equal.

What do you think is the type of class instance? >>>

```
>>> class Dog:
... pass
...
>>> a = Dog ()
>>> type (a)
<class '__main__.Dog'>
```

Let's look at the more complex example ...

```
class Dog:

    # Class Attribute
    species = 'mammal'

    # Initializer / Instance Attributes
    def __init__(self, name, age):
        self.name = name
        self.age = age


# Instantiate the Dog object
philo = Dog("Philo", 5)
mikey = Dog("Mikey", 6)

# Access the instance attributes
print("{} is {} and {} is {}.".format(
    philo.name, philo.age, mikey.name, mikey.age))

# Is Philo a mammal?
if philo.species == "mammal":
    print("{0} is a {1}!".format(philo.name, philo.species))
```

NOTE Notice how we use point records to access the attributes of each objects. Save as (dog_class.py), then run program. You should see:

```
Philo is 5 and Mikey is 6.
Philo is a mammal!
```

What's the matter?

We create a new instance of the Dog()class and assigned it to a variable Philo. Then we passed him two arguments, "Philo" and 5, which represent the name and age of this dog, respectively. These attribute are pass to the init method, which is called every time you creates a new attaching, instance the name and age to the object. You may be wondering why we should not have given self arguments.

This is the magic of Python: when you create a new instance of the class, Python automatically determines what selfies (in this case, Dog), and passes it to the init method.

Review of exercises (# 1)

Exercise: "The oldest dog"

Using the same Dogclass, create three new dogs, each with a different age. Then write a function with a name get_biggest_number()that takes any number of ages (*args) and returns the oldest. Then print the age of the oldest dog something like this:

 The oldest dog is 7 years old. Solution: "The oldest dog"

Solution "The oldest dog."

```
class Dog:

    # Class Attribute
    species = 'mammal'

    # Initializer / Instance Attributes
    def __init__(self, name, age):
        self.name = name
        self.age = age


# Instantiate the Dog object
jake = Dog("Jake", 7)
doug = Dog("Doug", 4)
william = Dog("William", 5)


# Determine the oldest dog
def get_biggest_number(*args):
    return max(args)


# Output
print("The oldest dog is {} years old.".format(
    get_biggest_number(jake.age, doug.age, william.age)))
```

Instance Methods

Instance methods are defined inside the class and are used to get the contents of the instance. They can also be used to perform operation with the attribute of our objects. Like a init method, the first argument is always self:

```
class Dog:

    # Class Attribute
    species = 'mammal'

    # Initializer / Instance Attributes
    def __init__(self, name, age):
        self.name = name
        self.age = age

    # instance method
    def description (self):
        return "{} is {} years old".format (self.name, self.age)

    # instance method
    def speak (self, sound):
        return "{} says {}".format (self.name, sound)

# Instantiate the Dog object
mikey = Dog ("Mikey", 6)

# call our instance methods
print (mikey.description ())
print (mikey.speak ("Gruff Gruff"))
```

Save as dog_instance_methods.py , then run it:

```
Mikey is 6 years old
Mikey says Gruff Gruff
```

In the last method, speak()we define the behavior. What other types of behavior can you assign to a dog? Go back to the beginning of the paragraph to see examples of the behavior of other objects.

Attribute Change

You can changes the value of attributes based on some behavior:

>>>

```
>>> class Email:
... def __init__ (self):
... self.is_sent = False
... def send_email (self):
... self.is_sent = True
...
>>> my_email = Email ()
>>> my_email.is_sent
False
>>> my_email.send_email ()
>>> my_email.is_sent
True
```

Here we added a method for sending an email that updates the
is_sentvariable to True.

Python object inheritance

Inheritance is a processing in which one class accepts the
attributes and methods of another. Newly created classes are
called child classes, and the classes from which the child classes
derive are called parent classes.

It is importants to note that child classes override or extend the
functionality (for example, attributes and behavior) of parent
classes. In other words, child classes inherit all the attributes and
behavior of the parent, but can also define other behavior to be
followed. The most basic type of class is the class object, which
usually all other classes inherit as the parents.

When you defining a new class, Python 3 implicitly uses its object
as the parent class. Thus, the following two definitions are
equivalent:

```
class Dog (object):
    pass

# In Python 3, this is the same as:

class Dog:
    pass
```

Note. In Python 2.x, there is a difference between the new and old-style classes. I will not go into details, but you will usually want to specify an object as the parent class to make sure that you define a new style class if you are writing Python 2 OOP code.

Dog Park Example

Let's imagine that we are in a dog park. There are several Dog objects involved in Dog behavior, each with different attributes. In ordinary conversation, this means that some dogs are running, and some are stretched, and some are just watching other dogs. Besides, each dog was named its owner, and since each dog lives and breathes, each is aging.

How else can you distinguish one dog from another? How about a dog breed: >>>

```
>>> class Dog:
...     def __init__(self, breed):
...     self.breed = breed
...
>>> spencer = Dog ("German Shepard")
>>> spencer.breed
'German Shepard'
>>> sara = Dog ("Boston Terrier")
>>> sara.breed
'Boston Terrier'
```

Each dog breed has slightly different behaviors. To take this into account, let's create separate classes for each breed. These are child classes of the parent Dogclass.

Extending parent class functionality

Create new file this called dog_inheritance.py :

```python
# Parent class
class Dog:

    # Class attribute
    species = 'mammal'

    # Initializer / Instance attributes
    def __init__(self, name, age):
        self.name = name
        self.age = age

    # instance method
    def description(self):
        return "{} is {} years old".format(self.name, self.age)

    # instance method
    def speak(self, sound):
        return "{} says {}".format(self.name, sound)


# Child class (inherits from Dog class)
class RussellTerrier(Dog):
    def run(self, speed):
        return "{} runs {}".format(self.name, speed)


# Child class (inherits from Dog class)
class Bulldog(Dog):
    def run(self, speed):
        return "{} runs {}".format(self.name, speed)


# Child classes inherit attributes and
# behaviors from the parent class
jim = Bulldog("Jim", 12)
print(jim.description())

# Child classes have specific attributes
# and behaviors as well
print(jim.run("slowly"))
```

Read the comments aloud while you are working with this program to help you understand what is happening, and then, before you run the program, see if you can predict the expected result.

You should see:

```
Jim is 12 years old
Jim runs slowly
```

We did not add any special attributes or methods to distinguish between a RussellTerrierand a Bulldog. Still, since they are now two different classes, we could, for example, give them different class attributes that determine their respective speeds.

Parent and child classes

isinstance()The function is used to determine if the instance is also an instance of a specific parent class. Save this as dog_isinstance.py :

```python
# Parent class
class Dog:

    # Class attribute
    species = 'mammal'

    # Initializer / Instance attributes
    def __init__(self, name, age):
        self.name = name
        self.age = age

    # instance method
    def description(self):
        return "{} is {} years old".format(self.name, self.age)

    # instance method
    def speak(self, sound):
        return "{} says {}".format(self.name, sound)


# Child class (inherits from Dog() class)
class RussellTerrier(Dog):
    def run(self, speed):
        return "{} runs {}".format(self.name, speed)


# Child class (inherits from Dog() class)
class Bulldog(Dog):
    def run(self, speed):
        return "{} runs {}".format(self.name, speed)


# Child classes inherit attributes and
# behaviors from the parent class
jim = Bulldog("Jim", 12)
print(jim.description())

# Child classes have specific attributes
# and behaviors as well
print(jim.run("slowly"))

# Is jim an instance of Dog()?
print(isinstance(jim, Dog))

# Is julie an instance of Dog()?
julie = Dog("Julie", 100)
print(isinstance(julie, Dog))

# Is johnny walker an instance of Bulldog()
johnnywalker = RussellTerrier("Johnny Walker", 4)
print(isinstance(johnnywalker, Bulldog))

# Is julie and instance of jim?
print(isinstance(julie, jim))
```

Conclusion: >>>

```
('Jim', 12)
Jim runs slowly
True
True
False
Traceback (most recent call last):
  File "dog_isinstance.py", line 50, in <module>
    print (isinstance (julie, jim))
TypeError: isinstance () arg 2 must be a class, type, or tuple of classes and types
```

It makes sense? Both jimand julieare instances of the Dog()class and johnnywalkerare not instances of Bulldog()the class. Then, as a health check, we checked juliewhether the instance is an instance jim, which is impossible, since jimit instancedoes not belong to the class itself, but to the class TypeError.

Overriding parent class functionality

Remember that child classes can also override the attributes and behavior of the parent class. For example: >>>

```
>>> class Dog:
... species = 'mammal'
...
>>> class SomeBreed (Dog):
... pass
...
>>> class SomeOtherBreed (Dog):
... species = 'reptile'
...
>>> frank = SomeBreed ()
>>> frank.species 'mammal'
>>> beans = SomeOtherBreed ()
>>> beans.species 'reptile'
```
The SomeBreed()class inherits speciesfrom the parent class, while the SomeOtherBreed()class overrides speciesby setting it reptile.

Review of exercises (# 2)

Exercise: "Legacy of the dogs"

Create a Petsclass that contains dog instances: this class is completely separate from the Dogclass. In other words, a Dogclass is not inherited from the Petsclass. Then assign three instances of the dog to the Petsclass instance . Start with the following code below. Save the file as pets_class.py . Your output should look like this:

```
I have 3 dogs.
Tom is 6.
Fletcher is 7.
Larry is 9.
And they're all mammals, of course.
```

Start Code:

```python
# Parent class
class Dog:

    # Class attribute
    species = 'mammal'

    # Initializer / Instance attributes
    def __init__(self, name, age):
        self.name = name
        self.age = age

    # instance method
    def description(self):
        return "{} is {} years old".format(self.name, self.age)

    # instance method
    def speak(self, sound):
        return "{} says {}".format(self.name, sound)

# Child class (inherits from Dog class)
class RussellTerrier(Dog):
    def run(self, speed):
        return "{} runs {}".format(self.name, speed)

# Child class (inherits from Dog class)
class Bulldog(Dog):
    def run(self, speed):
        return "{} runs {}".format(self.name, speed)
```

Solution: "Dog Inheritance"

```python
# Parent class
class Pets:

    dogs = []

    def __init__(self, dogs):
        self.dogs = dogs


# Parent class
class Dog:

    # Class attribute
    species = 'mammal'

    # Initializer / Instance attributes
    def __init__(self, name, age):
        self.name = name
        self.age = age

    # Instance method
    def description(self):
        return self.name, self.age

    # Instance method
    def speak(self, sound):
        return "%s says %s" % (self.name, sound)
```

```
# Instance method
def eat (self):
    self.is_hungry = False


# Child class (inherits from Dog class)
class RussellTerrier (Dog):
    def run (self, speed):
        return "%s runs%s s" % (self.name, speed)


# Child class (inherits from Dog class)
class Bulldog (Dog):
    def run (self, speed):
        return "%s runs%s s" % (self.name, speed)

# Create instances of dogs
my_dogs = [
    Bulldog ("Tom", 6),
    RussellTerrier ("Fletcher", 7),
    Dog ("Larry", 9)
]

# Instantiate the Pets class
my_pets = Pets (my_dogs)

# Output
print ("I have {} dogs.". format (len (my_pets.dogs)))
for dog in my_pets.dogs:
    print (" {} is {}.". format (dog.name, dog.age))

print ("And they're all {} s, of course.". format (dog.species))
```

Exercise: Hungry Dogs

Use the same files, add an instance attribute is_hungry = Truein

the Dogclass. Then add the called method, eat()which when

called changes the value is_hungryto False. Find out how best to

feed each dog, and then print "My dogs are hungry." if everyone

is hungry or "My dogs are not hungry." if everyone is not hungry.

The final result should look like this:

```
I have 3 dogs.
Tom is 6.
Fletcher is 7.
Larry is 9.
And they're all mammals, of course.
My dogs are not hungry.
```

Solution: Hungry Dogs

```
# Parent class
class Pets:

  dogs = []

  def __init__(self, dogs):
    self.dogs = dogs


# Parent class

  class Dog:

    * Oass attribute
    sped es = 'mamm d'

    * Initi d i zer." In stance attributes
    def iriit (self name age).
      self.name = name
      self.age = age
      self.is hungo.' = True

  = mist ance method
    def descripti on (self).
      return self.name self.age

  = mist ance method
    def speak (self sound).
      return " °. o s says°. o s" °. o (self.name sound)
```

```
= mist ance method
    def eat (self).
        self.is  hungo.'  =  Fdse


= Oiild class (inherits from Dog cl ass)
class RussellT erri er (Dog).
    def run (self speed).
        return " °. o s runs°. o s" °. o (self.name speedt


= Oiild class (inherits from Dog cl ass)
class Bulldog (Dog.
    def run (self speed).
        return " °. o s runs°. o s" °. o (self.name speedt

= Create instances of dogs
m\' dogs = [
    Bulldog (" Tom" 6)
    Ru ssellT erri er (" FI ct cher" Ti
    Dog ("L are.'" 9)


        stanttate the Pets class
ate'    ts = Pets (ate' dogs)

= Output
print (" I have { ) dogs.". format (len (m\'    ets.dogs)))
for dog in m\'    ets.dogs.
    dog.eat Q
    print (" { ) is { ).". format (dog.name dog.age))

print ("And the\"'re d1 { ) s of ccxirse." . format (dog.species))

are m\' dogs hungo.'  = Fdse
for dog in m\'    ets.dogs.
    if dog.i s  hungo.'.




are_my_dogs_hungry = True

if are_my_dogs_hungry:
    print ("My dogs are hungry.")
else:
    print ("My dogs are not hungry.")
```

Exercise: "Dog Walking"

Next, add a walk()method like Petsand Dogclasses, so that when you call a method in the Petsclass, each instance of a dog is assigned to Petsa class walk(). Save this as dog_walking.py . This is a little trickier.

Start by implementing a method just like a speak()method. As for the method in the Petsclass, you will need to iterate over the list of dogs and then call the method itself.

The output should look like this:

```
Tom is walking!
Fletcher is walking!
Larry is walking!
```

Solution: "dog walking"

```python
# Parent class
class Pets:

    dogs = []

    def __init__(self, dogs):
        self.dogs = dogs

    def walk(self):
        for dog in self.dogs:
            print(dog.walk())


# Parent class
class Dog:

    # Class attribute
    species = 'mammal'
    is_hungry = True

    # Initializer / Instance attributes
    def __init__(self, name, age):
        self.name = name
        self.age = age

    # Instance method
    def description(self):
        return self.name, self.age

    # Instance method
    def speak(self, sound):
        return "%s says% s" % (self.name, sound)

    # Instance method
    def eat(self):
        self.is_hungry = False
```

```
def walk (self):
    return "% s is walking!" % (self.name)

# Child class (inherits from Dog class)
class RussellTerrier (Dog):
    def run (self, speed):
        return "% s runs% s" % (self.name, speed)

# Child class (inherits from Dog class)
class Bulldog (Dog):
    def run (self, speed):
        return "% s runs% s" % (self.name, speed)

# Create instances of dogs
my_dogs = [
    Bulldog ("Tom", 6),
    RussellTerrier ("Fletcher", 7),
    Dog ("Larry", 9)
]

# Instantiate the Pet class
my_pets = Pets (my_dogs)

# Output
my_pets.walk ()
```

Exercise: "Testing Understanding"

Answer the following OOP questions to verify your learning progress:

What class?

What an example?

What is the relationship between class and instance?

What Python syntax is used to define a new class?

What is the spelling convention for a class name?

How do you create or create an instance of a class?

How do you access the attributes and behavior of an instance of a class?

What kind of method?

What is the purpose self?

What is the purpose of the init method?

Describe how inheritance helps prevent code duplication.

Can child classes override the properties of their parents?

Solution: "Test of understanding" Show hide

A class mechanism used to create new custom data structures. It contains data, as well as methods used to process this data.

An instance is a copy of a class with actual values, literally an object of a particular class.

While a class is a plan used to describe how to create something, instances are objects created from these drawings.

class PythonClassName:

Capitalized CamelCase designation - i.e. PythonClassName()

You use the class name followed by parentheses. So if the name of the class Dog(), the instance of the dog will be - my_class = Dog().

With dot notation - for example, instance_name.attribute_name

A function that defined inside a class.

The first argument of each method refers to the current instance of the class, which is called by the convention self. The init method self refers to a newly created object, while in other methods, it a self refers into the instance whose method was called. For more on the init con self, check out this article.

init The method initializes an instance of the class.

Child classes inherit all the attributes and behavior of the parent.

Yes.

Conclusion

Now you should know what classes are, why you want or should use them, and how to create parent and child classes to better structure your programs.

Remember that OOP is a programming paradigm, not a Python concept. Most modern programming languages, such as Java, C #, C ++, follow the principles of OOP. So the good news is that learning the basics of object-oriented programming will be useful to you in a variety of circumstances - whether you work in Python or not.

Now the industry does not stand still and there are more and more web sites, services and companies that need specialists. Demand for developers is growing, but competition among them is growing.

To be the best in your business, you need to be almost an absolutely universal person who can write a website, create a design for it, and promote it yourself.

In this regard, even a person who has never sat at this computer begins to think, but should I try?

But very often it turns out that such enthusiasts burn out at the initial stage, without having tried themselves in this matter.

Or maybe he would become a brilliant creator of code? Would create something new? This we will not know.

Every day, the threshold for entering programming is growing. You can never predict what new language will come out.

Such an abundance breaks all the desire of a newly minted programmer and he is lost in this ocean of information.

All these javascripts of yours ... pythons ... what fear ..

A great misconception is the obligation to know mathematics. Yes, it is needed, but only in a narrow field, but it is also useful for understanding some aspects.

The advice that can be given to people who are just starting their activity is not to chase everything at once. Allow yourself time to think.

What do I want to do? Create a program for everyone to be useful? Create additional services to simplify any tasks? Or do you really have to go make games?

The second advice will be to answer my question how much time am I ready to devote to this? The third point is to think about how fast you want to achieve your intended result.

So, there is no "easy way" to start programming, it all depends on you - your interest, what you want to do and your tasks.

In any case, you need to try and do everything possible in your power. Good luck in your endeavors!

PYTHON FOR

DATA SCIENCE

Guide to computer programming and web coding. Learn machine learning, artificial intelligence, NumPy and Pandas packages for data analysis. Step-by-step exercises included.

JASON TEST

Introduction

Data Science has been very popular over the last couple of years. The main focus of this sector is to incorporate significant data into business and marketing strategies that will help a business expand. And get to a logical solution, the data can be stored and explored. Originally only the leading IT corporations were engaged throughout this field, but today information technology is being used by companies operating in different sectors and fields such as e-commerce, medical care, financial services, and others. Software processing programs such as Hadoop, R code, SAS, SQL, and plenty more are available. Python is, however, the most famous and easiest to use data and analytics tools. It is recognized as the coding world's Swiss Army Knife since it promotes structured coding, object-oriented programming, the operational programming language, and many others. Python is the most widely used programming language in the world and is also recognized as the most high - level language for data science tools and techniques, according to the 2018 Stack Overflow study.

In the Hacker rank 2018 developer poll, which is seen in their love-hate ranking, Python has won the developer's hearts. Experts in data science expect to see an increase in the Python ecosystem, with growing popularity. And although your journey to study Python programming may just start, it's nice to know that there are also plentiful (and increasing) career options. Data analytics Python programming is extensively used and, along with being a flexible and open-source language, becomes one of the favorite programming languages. Its large libraries are used for data processing, and even for a beginner data analyst, they are very easy to understand. Besides being open-source, it also integrates easily with any infrastructure that can be used to fix the most complicated problems. It is used by most banks for data crunching, organizations for analysis and processing, and weather prediction firms such as Climate monitor analytics often use it. The annual wage for a Computer Scientist is $127,918, according to Indeed. So here's the good news, the figure is likely to increase. IBM's experts forecast a 28 percent increase in data scientists' demands by 2020. For data science, however, the future is bright, and Python is just one slice of the golden pie. Luckily mastering Python and other principles of programming are as practical as ever.

DATA SCIENCE AND ITS SIGNIFICANCE

Data Science has come a long way from the past few years, and thus, it becomes an important factor in understanding the workings of multiple companies. Below are several explanations that prove data science will still be an integral part of the global market.

1. The companies would be able to understand their client in a more efficient and high manner with the help of Data Science. Satisfied customers form the foundation of every company, and they play an important role in their successes or failures. Data Science allows companies to engage with customers in the advance way and thus proves the product's improved performance and strength.

2. Data Science enables brands to deliver powerful and engaging visuals. That's one of the reasons it's famous. When products and companies make inclusive use of this data, they can share their experiences with their audiences and thus create better relations with the item.

3. Perhaps one Data Science's significant characteristics are that its results can be generalized to almost all kinds of industries, such as travel, health care, and education. The companies can

quickly determine their problems with the help of Data Science, and can also adequately address them

4. Currently, data science is accessible in almost all industries, and nowadays, there is a huge amount of data existing in the world, and if used adequately, it can lead to victory or failure of any project. If data is used properly, it will be important in the future to achieve the product 's goals.

5. Big data is always on the rise and growing. Big data allows the enterprise to address complicated Business, human capital, and capital management problems effectively and quickly using different resources that are built routinely.

6. Data science is gaining rapid popularity in every other sector and therefore plays an important role in every product's functioning and performance. Thus, the data scientist's role is also enhanced as they will conduct an essential function of managing data and providing solutions to particular issues.

7. Computer technology has also affected the supermarket sectors. To understand this, let's take an example the older people had a fantastic interaction with the local seller. Also, the seller was able to meet the customers' requirements in a personalized way. But now this attention was lost due to the emergence and increase of supermarket chains. But the sellers are able to communicate with their customers with the help of data analytics.

8. Data Science helps companies build that customer connection. Companies and their goods will be able to have a better and deeper understanding of how clients can utilize their services with the help of data science.

Data Technology Future: Like other areas are continually evolving, the importance of data technology is increasingly growing as well. Data science impacted different fields. Its influence can be seen in many industries, such as retail, healthcare, and education. New treatments and technologies are being continually identified in the healthcare sector, and there is a need for quality patient care. The healthcare industry can find a solution with the help of data science techniques that helps the patients to take care with. Education is another field where one can clearly see the advantage of data science. Now the new innovations like phones and tablets have become an essential characteristic of the educational system. Also, with the help of data science, the students are creating greater chances, which leads to improving their knowledge.

Data Science Life Cycle:

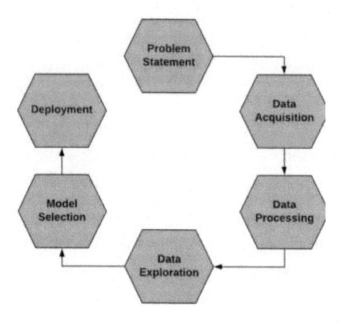

Data Structures

A data structure may be selected in computer programming or designed to store data for the purpose of working with different algorithms on it. Every other data structure includes the data values, data relationships, and functions between the data that can be applied to the data and information.

Features of data structures

Sometimes, data structures are categorized according to their characteristics. Possible functions are:

Linear or non-linear: This feature defines how the data objects are organized in a sequential series, like a list or in an unordered sequence, like a table.

Homogeneous or non-homogeneous: This function defines how all data objects in a collection are of the same type or of different kinds.

Static or dynamic: This technique determines to show to assemble the data structures. Static data structures at compilation time have fixed sizes, structures, and destinations in the memory. Dynamic data types have dimensions, mechanisms, and destinations of memory that may shrink or expand depending on the application.

Data structure Types

Types of the data structure are determined by what sorts of operations will be needed or what kinds of algorithms will be implemented. This includes:

Arrays: An array stores a list of memory items at adjacent locations. Components of the same category are located together since each element's position can be easily calculated or accessed. Arrays can be fixed in size or flexible in length.

Stacks: A stack holds a set of objects in linear order added to operations. This order may be past due in first out (LIFO) or first-out (FIFO).

Queues: A queue stores a stack-like selection of elements; however, the sequence of activity can only be first in the first out. Linked lists: In a linear order, a linked list stores a selection of items. In a linked list, every unit or node includes a data item as well as a reference or relation to the next element in the list.

Trees: A tree stocks an abstract, hierarchical collection of items. Each node is connected to other nodes and can have several sub-values, also known as a child.

Graphs: A graph stores a non-linear design group of items. Graphs consist of a limited set of nodes, also called vertices, and lines connecting them, also known as edges. They are useful for describing processes in real life, such as networked computers.

Tries: A tria or query tree is often a data structure that stores strings as data files, which can be arranged in a visual graph.

Hash tables: A hash table or hash chart is contained in a relational list that labels the keys to variables. A hash table uses a hashing algorithm to transform an index into an array of containers containing the desired item of data. These data systems are called complex because they can contain vast quantities of interconnected data. Examples of primal, or fundamental, data structures are integer, float, boolean, and character.

Utilization of data structures

Data structures are generally used to incorporate the data types in physical forms. This can be interpreted into a wide range of applications, including a binary tree showing a database table. Data structures are used in the programming languages to organize code and information in digital storage. Python databases and dictionaries, or JavaScript array and objects, are popular coding systems used to gather and analyze data. Also, data structures are a vital part of effective software design. Significance of Databases Data systems is necessary to effectively handle vast volumes of data, such as data stored in libraries, or indexing services.

Accurate data configuration management requires memory allocation identifier, data interconnections, and data processes, all of which support the data structures. In addition, it is important to not only use data structures but also to select the correct data structure for each assignment.

Choosing an unsatisfactory data structure could lead to slow running times or disoriented code. Any considerations that need to be noticed when choosing a data system include what type of information should be processed, where new data will be put, how data will be organized, and how much space will be allocated for the data.

PYTHON BASICS

You can get all the knowledge about the Python programming language in 5 simple steps.

Step 1: Practice Basics in Python
It all starts somewhere. This first step is where the basics of programming Python will be learned. You are always going to want an introduction to data science. Jupyter Notebook, which comes pre-portioned with Python libraries to help you understand these two factors, which make it one of the essential resources which you can start using early on your journey.

Step 2: Try practicing Mini-Python Projects
We strongly believe in learning through shoulders-on. Try programming stuff like internet games, calculators, or software that gets Google weather in your area. Creating these mini-projects can help you understand Python. Projects like these are standard for any coding languages, and a fantastic way to strengthen your working knowledge. You will come up with better and advance API knowledge, and you will continue site scraping with advanced techniques. This will enable you to learn

Python programming more effectively, and the web scraping method will be useful to you later when collecting data.

Stage 3: Learn Scientific Libraries on Python

Python can do anything with data. Pandas, Matplotliband, and NumPyare are known to be the three best used and most important Python Libraries for data science. NumPy and Pandas are useful for data creation and development. Matplotlib is a library for analyzing the data, creating flow charts and diagrams as you would like to see in Excel or Google Sheets.

Stage 4: Create a portfolio

A portfolio is an absolute need for professional data scientists. These projects must include numerous data sets and leave important perspectives to readers that you have gleaned. Your portfolio does not have a specific theme; finding datasets that inspire you, and then finding a way to place them together. Showing projects like these provide some collaboration to fellow data scientists, and demonstrates future employers that you have really taken the chance to understand Python and other essential coding skills. Some of the good things about data science are that, while showcasing the skills you've learned, your portfolio serves as a resume, such as Python programming.

Step 5: Apply Advanced Data Science Techniques

Eventually, the target is to strengthen your programming skills. Your data science path will be full of continuous learning, but you can accomplish specialized tutorials to make sure you have specialized in the basic programming of Python. You need to get confident with clustering models of regression, grouping, and k-means. You can also leap into machine learning-using sci-kit lessons to bootstrap models and create neural network models. At this point, developer programming could include creating models using live data sources. This type of machine learning technique adjusts s its assumptions over time.

How significant is Python for Data Science?

Efficient and simple to use – Python is considered a tool for beginners, and any student or researcher with only basic understanding could start working on it. Time and money spent debugging codes and constraints on different project management are also minimized. The time for code implementation is less compared to other programming languages such as C, Java, and C #, which makes developers and software engineers spend far more time working on their algorithms.

Library Choice-Python offers a vast library and machine learning and artificial intelligence database. Scikit Learn, TensorFlow, Seaborn, Pytorch, Matplotlib, and many more are among the most popular libraries. There are many online tutorial

videos and resources on machine learning and data science, which can be easily obtained.

Scalability – Python has proven itself to be a highly scalable and faster language compared to other programming languages such as c++, Java, and R. It gives flexibility in solving problems that can't be solved with other computer languages. Many companies use it to develop all sorts of rapid techniques and systems.

#Visual Statistics and Graphics-Python provides a number of visualization tools. The Matplotlib library provides a reliable framework on which those libraries such as gg plot, pandas plotting, PyTorch, and others are developed. These services help create graphs, plot lines ready for the Web, visual layouts, etc.

How Python is used for Data Science

#First phase – First of all, we need to learn and understand what form a data takes. If we perceive data to be a huge Excel sheet with columns and crows lakhs, then perhaps you should know what to do about that? You need to gather information into each row as well as column by executing some operations and searching for a specific type of data. Completing this type of computational task can consume a lot of time and hard work. Thus, you can use Python's libraries, such as Pandas and Numpy, that can complete the tasks quickly by using parallel computation.

#Second phase – The next hurdle is to get the data needed. Since data is not always readily accessible to us, we need to dump data from the network as needed. Here the Python Scrap and brilliant Soup libraries can enable us to retrieve data from the internet.

#Third phase – We must get the simulation or visual presentation of the data at this step. Driving perspectives gets difficult when you have too many figures on the board. The correct way to do that is to represent the data in graph form, graphs, and other layouts. The Python Seaborn and Matplotlib libraries are used to execute this operation.

#Fourth phase – The next stage is machine-learning, which is massively complicated computing. It includes mathematical tools such as the probability, calculus, and matrix operations of columns and rows over lakhs. With Python's machine learning library Scikit-Learn, all of this will become very simple and effective.

Standard Library

The Python Standard library consists of Python's precise syntax, token, and semantic. It comes packaged with deployment core Python. When we started with an introduction, we referenced this. It is written in C and covers features such as I / O and other core components. Together all of the versatility renders makes Python the language it is. At the root of the basic library, there are more than 200 key modules. Python ships that library. But aside from this library, you can also obtain a massive collection of several thousand Python Package Index (PyPI) components.

1. Matplotlib

'Matplotlib' helps to analyze data, and is a library of numerical plots. For Data Science, we discussed in Python.

2. Pandas

'Pandas' is a must for data-science as we have said before. It provides easy, descriptive, and versatile data structures to deal with organized (tabulated, multilayered, presumably heterogeneous) and series data with ease (and fluidly).

3. Requests

'Requests' is a Python library that allows users to upload HTTP/1.1 requests, add headers, form data, multipart files, and simple Python dictionary parameters. In the same way, it also helps you to access the response data.

4. NumPy

It has basic arithmetic features and a rudimentary collection of scientific computing.

5. SQLAlchemy

It has sophisticated mathematical features, and SQLAlchemy is a basic mathematical programming library with well-known trends at a corporate level. It was created to make database availability efficient and high-performance.

6. BeautifulSoup

This may be a bit on the slow side. BeautifulSoup seems to have a superb library for beginner XML- and HTML- parsing.

7. Pyglet

Pyglet is an outstanding choice when designing games with an object-oriented programming language interface. It also sees use in the development of other visually rich programs for Mac OS X, Windows, and Linux in particular. In the 90s, they turned to play Minecraft on their PCs whenever people were bored. Pyglet is the mechanism powering Minecraft.

8. SciPy

Next available is SciPy, one of the libraries we spoke about so often. It does have a range of numerical routines that are user-friendly and effective. Those provide optimization routines and numerical integration procedures.

9. Scrapy

If your objective is quick, scraping at the high-level monitor and crawling the network, go for Scrapy. It can be used for data gathering activities for monitoring and test automation.

10. PyGame

PyGame offers an incredibly basic interface to the system-independent graphics, audio, and input libraries of the Popular Direct Media Library (SDL).

11. Python Twisted

Twisted is an event-driven networking library used in Python and authorized under the MIT open-source license.

12. Pillow

Pillow is a PIL (Python Imaging Library) friendly fork but is more user efficient. Pillow is your best friend when you're working with pictures.

13. pywin32

As the name suggests, this gives useful methods and classes for interacting with Windows.

14. wxPython

For Python, it's a wrapper around wxWidgets.

15. iPython

iPython Python Library provides a parallel distributed computing architecture. You will use it to create, run, test, and track parallel and distributed programming.

16. Nose

The nose provides alternate test exploration and test automation running processes. This intends to mimic the behavior of the py.test as much as possible.

17. Flask

Flask is a web framework, with a small core and several extensions.

18. SymPy

It is a library of open-source symbolic mathematics. SymPy is a full-fledged Computer Algebra System (CAS) with a very simple and easily understood code that is highly expandable. It is implemented in python, and therefore, external libraries are not required.

19. Fabric

As well as being a library, Fabric is a command-line tool to simplify the use of SSH for installation programs or network management activities. You can run local or remote command line, upload/download files, and even request input user going, or abort activity with it.

20. PyGTK

PyGTK allows you to create programs easily using a Python GUI (Graphical User Interface).

Operators and Expressions

Operators

In Python, operators are special symbols that perform mathematical operation computation. The value in which the operator is running on is called the operand.

Arithmetic operators

It is used by arithmetic operators to perform mathematical operations such as addition, subtraction, multiplying, etc.

Comparison operators

Comparison operators can be used for value comparisons. Depending on the condition, it returns either True or False.

Logical operators

Logical operators are and, or, not.

Operator	Meaning	Example
And	True if both operands are true	x and y
Or	True if either of the operands is true	x or y
Not	True if the operand is false (complements the operand)	not x

Bitwise operators

Bitwise operators operate as if they became binary-digit strings on operands. Bit by bit they work, and therefore the name. For example, in binary two is10, and in binary seven is 111.

Assignment operators

Python language's assignment operators are used to assign values to the variables. a = 5 is a simple task operator assigning 'a' value of 5 to the right of the variable 'a' to the left. In Python, there are various compound operators such as a + = 5, which adds to the variable as well as assigns the same later. This equals a= a + 5.

Special operators

Python language gives other different types of operators, such as the operator of the identity or the operator of membership. Examples of these are mentioned below.

Identity operators

'Is' and 'is not' are Python Identity Operators. They are used to test if there are two values or variables in the same memory section. Two equal variables do not mean they are equivalent.

Membership operator

The operators that are used to check whether or not there exists a value/variable in the sequence such as string, list, tuples, sets, and dictionary. These operators return either True or False if a variable is found in the list, it returns True, or else it returns False

Expressions

An expression is a mix of values, variables, operators, and function calls. There must be an evaluation of the expressions. When you ask Python to print a phrase, the interpreter will evaluate the expression and show the output.

Arithmetic conversions

Whenever an arithmetic operator interpretation below uses the phrase "the numeric arguments are converted to a common type," this means the execution of the operator for the built-in modes operates as follows

If one argument is a complex quantity, then the other is converted to a complex number; If another argument is a floating-point number, the other argument is transformed to a floating-point; Or else both will be integers with no need for conversion.

Atoms

Atoms are the most important expressional components. The smallest atoms are literals or abstract identities. Forms contained in parentheses, brackets, or braces are also syntactically known as atoms. Atoms syntax is:

atom ::= identifier | enclosure| literal

enclosure ::= list_display| parenth_form| dict_display |
set_display

Identifiers (Names)

A name is an identifier that occurs as an atom. See section
Lexical Description Identifiers and Keywords and group Naming
and binding for naming and binding documents. Whenever the
name is connected to an entity, it yields the entity by evaluating
the atom. When a name is not connected, an attempt to assess it
elevates the exception for NameError.

Literals

Python provides logical string and bytes and numerical literals of
different types:
literal::= string literal | bytes literal
         | integer | float number | image number
Assessment of a literal yield with the predicted set an object of
that type (bytes, integer, floating-point number, string, complex
number). In the scenario of floating-point and imaginary
(complex) literals, the value can be approximated.

Parenthesized forms

A parenthesized type is an available set of parentheses for the expression:

parenth_form ::= "(" [starred_expression] ")"

A list of parenthesized expressions yields whatever the list of expressions produces: if the list includes at least one comma, it produces a tuple. If not, it yields the sole expression that forms up the list of expressions. A null pair of parentheses generates an incomplete object of tuples. As all tuples are immutable, the same rules would apply as for literals (i.e., two empty tuple occurrences does or doesn't yield the same entity).

Displays for lists, sets, and dictionaries

For the construction of a list, Python uses a series or dictionary with a particular syntax called "displays," each in complementary strands:

The contents of the container are listed explicitly, or They are calculated using a series of instructions for looping and filtering, named a 'comprehension.' Common features of syntax for comprehensions are:

comprehension ::= assignment_expressioncomp_for

comp_for   ::= ["async"] "for" target_list "in" or_test [comp_iter]

comp_iter   ::= comp_for | comp_if

comp_if   ::= "if" expression_nocond [comp_iter]

A comprehension contains one single sentence ready for at least one expression for clause, and zero or more for or if clauses. Throughout this situation, the components of the container are those that will be generated by assuming each of the for or if clauses as a block, nesting from left to right, and determining the phase for creating an entity each time the inner core block is approached.

List displays

A list view is a probably empty sequence of square brackets including expressions:

list_display ::= "[" [starred_list | comprehension] "]"

A list display generates a new column object, with either a list of expressions or a comprehension specifying the items. When a comma-separated database of expressions is provided, its elements are assessed from left to right and positioned in that order in the category entity. When Comprehension is provided, the list shall be built from the comprehension components.

Set displays

Curly braces denote a set display and can be distinguished from dictionary displays by the lack of colons dividing data types:

set_display ::= "{" (starred_list | comprehension) "}"

A set show offers a new, mutable set entity, with either a series of expressions or a comprehension defining the contents. When supplied with a comma-separated list of expressions, its elements are evaluated from left to right and assigned to the set entity. Whenever a comprehension is provided, the set is formed from the comprehension-derived elements. Unable to build an empty set with this {}; literal forms a blank dictionary.

Dictionary displays

A dictionary view is a potentially empty sequence of key pairs limited to curly braces:

dict_display   ::= "{" [key_datum_list | dict_comprehension] "}"

key_datum_list   ::= key_datum ("," key_datum)* [","]

key_datum   ::= expression ":" expression | "**" or_expr

dict_comprehension ::= expression ":" expression comp_for

The dictionary view shows a new object in the dictionary. When a comma-separated series of key / datum pairs is provided, they are analyzed from left to right to identify dictionary entries: each key entity is often used as a key to hold the respective datum in the dictionary. This implies you can clearly state the very same key numerous times in the key /datum catalog, but the last one given will become the final dictionary's value for that key.

Generator expressions

A generator expression is the compressed syntax of a generator in the parenthesis :

generator_expression ::= "(" expression comp_for ")"

An expression generator produces an entity that is a new generator. Its syntax will be the same as for comprehensions, except for being enclosed in brackets or curly braces rather than parentheses. Variables being used generator expression are assessed sloppily when the generator object (in the same style as standard generators) is called by the __next__() method. Conversely, the iterate-able expression in the leftmost part of the clause is evaluated immediately, such that an error that it produces is transmitted at the level where the expression of the generator is characterized, rather than at the level where the first value is recovered.

For instance: (x*y for x in range(10) for y in range(x, x+10)).

Yield expressions

yield_atom   ::= "(" yield_expression ")"

yield_expression ::= "yield" [expression_list | "from" expression]

The produced expression is used to define a generator function or async generator function, and can therefore only be used in the function definition body. Using an expression of yield in the body of a function tends to cause that function to be a generator, and to use it in the body of an asynchronous def function induces that co-routine function to become an async generator. For example:

```
def gen():  # defines a generator function
yield 123
asyncdefagen(): # defines an asynchronous generator function
yield 123
```

Because of their adverse effects on the carrying scope, yield expressions are not allowed as part of the impliedly defined scopes used to enforce comprehensions and expressions of generators.

Input and Output of Data in Python

Python Output Using print() function

To display data into the standard display system (screen), we use the print() function. We may issue data to a server as well, but that will be addressed later. Below is an example of its use.

```
>>>>print('This sentence is output to the screen')
```

Output:

This sentence is output to the screen

Another example is given:

```
a = 5
print('The value of a is,' a)
```

Output:

The value of a is 5

Within the second declaration of print(), we will note that space has been inserted between the string and the variable value a. By default, it contains this syntax, but we can change it.

The actual syntax of the print() function will be:

```
print(*objects, sep=' ', end='\n', file=sys.stdout, flush=False)
```

Here, the object is the value(s) that will be printed. The sep separator between values is used. This switches into a character in space. Upon printing all the values, the finish is printed. It moves into a new section by design. The file is the object that prints the values, and its default value is sys.stdout (screen). Below is an example of this.

```
print(1, 2, 3, 4)
print(1, 2, 3, 4, sep='*')
print(1, 2, 3, 4, sep='#', end='&')
```

Run code

Output:

```
1 2 3 4
1*2*3*4
```

Output formatting

Often we want to style our production, so it looks appealing. It can be done using the method str.format(). This technique is visible for any object with a string.

>>> x = 5; y = 10

>>>print('The value of x is {} and y is {}'.format(x,y))

Here the value of x is five and y is 10

Here, they use the curly braces{} as stand-ins. Using numbers (tuple index), we may specify the order in which they have been printed.

print('I love {0} and {1}'.format('bread','butter'))

print('I love {1} and {0}'.format('bread','butter'))

Run Code

Output:

I love bread and butter

I love butter and bread

People can also use arguments with keyword to format the string.

>>>print('Hello {name}, {greeting}'.format(greeting =
'Goodmorning', name = 'John'))

Hello John, Goodmorning

Unlike the old sprint() style used in the C programming language, we can also format strings. To accomplish this, we use the '%' operator.

```
>>> x = 12.3456789
>>>print('The value of x is %3.2f' %x)
The value of x is 12.35
>>>print('The value of x is %3.4f' %x)
The value of x is 12.3457
```

Python Indentation

Indentation applies to the spaces at the start of a line of the compiler. Whereas indentation in code is for readability only in other programming languages, but the indentation in Python is very important. Python supports the indent to denote a code block.

Example

```
if 5 > 2:
print("Five is greater than two!")
```

Python will generate an error message if you skip the indentation:

Example

Syntax Error:

```
if 5 > 2:
print("Five is greater than two!")
```

Python Input

Our programs have been static. Variables were described or hard-coded in the source code. We would want to take the feedback from the user to allow flexibility. We have the input() function in Python to enable this. input() is syntax as:

input([prompt])

While prompt is the string we want to show on the computer, this is optional.

```
>>>num = input('Enter a number: ')
Enter a number: 10
>>>num
'10'
```

Below, we can see how the value 10 entered is a string and not a number. To transform this to a number we may use the functions int() or float().

```
>>>int('10')
10
>>>float('10')
10.0
```

The same method can be done with the feature eval(). Although it takes eval much further. It can even quantify expressions, provided that the input is a string

```
>>>int('2+3')
Traceback (most recent call last):
  File "<string>", line 301, in runcode
  File "<interactive input>", line 1, in <module>
ValueError: int() base 10 invalid literal: '2+3'
>>>eval('2+3')
5
```

Python Import

As our software gets larger, splitting it up into separate modules is a smart idea. A module is a file that contains definitions and statements from Python. Python packages have a filename, and the .py extension begins with it. Definitions may be loaded into another module or to the integrated Python interpreter within a module. To do this, we use the keyword on import.

For instance, by writing the line below, we can import the math module:

import math

We will use the module as follows:

import math

print(math.pi)

Run Code

Output

3.141592653589793

So far, all concepts are included in our framework within the math module. Developers can also only import certain particular attributes and functions, using the keyword.

For instance:

```
>>>from math import pi
>>>pi
3.141592653589793
```

Python looks at multiple positions specified in sys.path during the import of a module. It is a list of positions in a directory.

```
>>> import sys
>>>sys.path
['',
 'C:\\Python33\\Lib\\idlelib',
 'C:\\Windows\\system32\\python33.zip',
 'C:\\Python33\\DLLs',
 'C:\\Python33\\lib',
 'C:\\Python33',
 'C:\\Python33\\lib\\site-packages']
```

We can insert our own destination to that list as well.

FUNCTIONS

You utilize programming functions to combine a list of instructions that you're constantly using or that are better self-contained in sub-program complexity and are called upon when required. Which means a function is a type of code written to accomplish a given purpose. The function may or may not need various inputs to accomplish that particular task. Whenever the task is executed, one or even more values can or could not be returned by the function. Basically there exist three types of functions in Python language:

Built-in functions, including help() to ask for help, min() to just get the minimum amount, print() to print an attribute to the terminal. More of these functions can be found here.

User-Defined Functions (UDFs) that are functions created by users to assist and support them out;

Anonymous functions, also labeled lambda functions since they are not defined with the default keyword.

Defining A Function: User Defined Functions (UDFs)

The following four steps are for defining a function in Python:

Keyword def can be used to declare the function and then use the function name to backtrack.

Add function parameters: They must be within the function parentheses. Finish off your line with a colon.

Add statements which should be implemented by the functions. When the function should output something, end your function with a return statement. Your task must return an object None without return declaration. Example:

```
def hello():
print("Hello World")
return
```

It is obvious as you move forward, the functions will become more complex: you can include for loops, flow control, and more to make things more fine-grained:

```
def hello():
name = str(input("Enter your name: "))
if name:
print ("Hello " + str(name))
else:
print("Hello World")
return
hello()
```

In the feature above, you are asking the user to give a name. When no name is provided, the 'Hello World' function will be printed. Otherwise, the user will receive a custom "Hello" phrase. Also, consider you can specify one or more parameters for your UDFs function. When you discuss the segment Feature Statements, you will hear more about this. Consequently, as a result of your function, you may or may not return one or more values.

The return Statement

Note that since you're going to print something like that in your hello) (UDF, you don't really have to return it. There'll be no distinction between the above function and this one:

Example:
1. defhello_noreturn():
2. print("Hello World")

Even so, if you'd like to keep working with the result of your function and try a few other functions on it, you'll need to use the return statement to simply return a value, like a string, an integer. Check out the following scenario in which hello() returns a "hello" string while the hello_noreturn() function returns None:

1.   def hello():

2.   print("Hello World")

3.   return("hello")

4.   defhello_noreturn():

5.   print("Hello World")

6.   # Multiply the output of `hello()` with 2

7.   hello() * 2

8.   # (Try to) multiply the output of `hello_noreturn()` with 2

9.   hello_noreturn() * 2

The secondary part gives you an error because, with a None, you cannot perform any operations. You will get a TypeError that appears to say that NoneType (the None, which is the outcome of hello_noreturn()) and int (2) cannot do the multiplication operation. Tip functions leave instantly when a return statement is found, even though that means they will not return any result:

1. def run():

2. for x in range(10):

3. if x == 2:

4. return

5. print("Run!")

6.   run()

Another factor worth noting when dealing with the 'return expression' is many values can be returned using it. You consider making use of tuples for this. Recall that this data structure is very comparable to a list's: it can contain different values. Even so, tuples are immutable, meaning you can't alter any amounts stored in it! You build it with the aid of dual parentheses). With the assistance of the comma and the assignment operator, you can disassemble tuples into different variables.

Read the example below to understand how multiple values can be returned by your function:

1. # Define `plus()`
2.   def plus(a,b):
3.sum = a + b
4.return (sum, a)

5. # Call `plus()` and unpack variables
6.   sum, a = plus(3,4)
7.   # Print `sum()`
8.   print(sum)

Notice that the return statement sum, 'a' will result in just the same as the return (sum, a): the earlier simply packs total and an in a tuple it under hood!

How To Call A Function

You've already seen a lot of examples in previous sections of how one can call a function. Trying to call a function means executing the function you have described-either directly from the Python prompt, or by a different function (as you have seen in the "Nested Functions" portion). Call your new added hello() function essentially by implementing hello() as in the DataCamp Light chunk as follows:

1.   hello()

Adding Docstrings to Python Functions

Further valuable points of Python's writing functions: docstrings. Docstrings define what your function does, like the algorithms it conducts or the values it returns. These definitions act as metadata for your function such that anybody who reads the docstring of your feature can understand what your feature is doing, without having to follow all the code in the function specification. Task docstrings are placed right after the feature header in the subsequent line and are set in triple quote marks. For your hello() function, a suitable docstring is 'Hello World prints.'

```
def hello():
"""Prints "Hello World".
Returns:
    None
```

```
"""
print("Hello World")
return
```

Notice that you can extend docstrings more than the one provided here as an example. If you want to study docstrings in more depth information, you should try checking out some Python library Github repositories like scikit-learn or pandas, in which you'll find lots of good examples!

Function Arguments in Python

You probably learned the distinction between definitions and statements earlier. In simple terms, arguments are the aspects that are given to any function or method call, while their parameter identities respond to the arguments in the function or method code. Python UDFs can take up four types of arguments:

Default arguments

Required arguments

Keyword arguments

Variable number of arguments

Default Arguments

Default arguments would be those who take default data if no value of the argument is delivered during the call function. With the assignment operator =, as in the following case, you may assign this default value:

1. #Define `plus()` function

2. def plus(a,b = 2):

3.return a + b

4. # Call `plus()` with only `a` parameter

5. plus(a=1)

6. # Call `plus()` with `a` and `b` parameters

7. plus(a=1, b=3)

Required Arguments

Because the name sort of brings out, the claims a UDF needs are those that will be in there. Such statements must be transferred during the function call and are absolutely the right order, such as in the example below:

1. # Define `plus()` with required arguments

2. def plus(a,b):

3. return a + b

Calling the functions without getting any additional errors, you need arguments that map to 'a' as well as the 'b' parameters. The result will not be unique if you swap round the 'a' and 'b,' but it could be if you modify plus() to the following:

1. # Define `plus()` with required arguments

2. def plus(a,b):

3.return a/b

Keyword Arguments

You will use keyword arguments in your function call if you'd like to make sure you list all the parameters in the correct order. You use this to define the statements by the name of the function. Let's take an example above to make it a little simpler:

1. # Define `plus()` function
2. def plus(a,b):
3.return a + b
4. # Call `plus()` function with parameters
5. plus(2,3)
6. # Call `plus()` function with keyword arguments
7. plus(a=1, b=2)

Notice that you can also alter the sequence of the parameters utilizing keywords arguments and still get the same outcome when executing the function:

1. # Define `plus()` function
2. def plus(a,b):
3.return a + b
4. # Call `plus()` function with keyword arguments
5. plus(b=2, a=1)

Global vs. Local Variables

Variables identified within a function structure usually have a local scope, and those specified outside have a global scope. This shows that the local variables are specified within a function block and can only be retrieved through that function, while global variables can be retrieved from all the functions in the coding:

1. # Global variable `init`
2. init = 1
3. # Define `plus()` function to accept a variable number of arguments
4. def plus(*args):
5. # Local variable `sum()`
6.total = 0
7.fori in args:
8.total += i
9.return total
10.# Access the global variable
11.print("this is the initialized value " + str(init))
12.# (Try to) access the local variable
13.print("this is the sum " + str(total))

You will find that you can get a NameError that means the name 'total' is not specified as you attempt to print out the total local variable that was specified within the body of the feature. In comparison, the init attribute can be written out without any complications.

Anonymous Functions in Python

Anonymous functions are often termed lambda functions in Python since you are using the lambda keyword rather than naming it with the standard-def keyword.

1. double = lambda x: x*2
2. double(5)

The anonymous or lambda feature in the DataCamp Light chunk above is lambda x: x*2. X is the argument, and x*2 is the interpretation or instruction that is analyzed and given back. What is unique about this function, and it has no tag, like the examples you saw in the first section of the lecture for this function. When you had to write the above function in a UDF, you would get the following result:

```
def double(x):
return x*2
```

Let us see another example of a lambda function where two arguments are used:

1. # `sum()` lambda function
2.   sum = lambda x, y: x + y;
3. # Call the `sum()` anonymous function
4.   sum(4,5)
5. # "Translate" to a UDF
6.   def sum(x, y):
7. returnx+y

When you need a function with no name for a short interval of time, you utilize anonymous functions and this is generated at runtime. Special contexts where this is important are when operating with filter(), map() and redu():

1. from functools import reduce
2. my_list = [1,2,3,4,5,6,7,8,9,10]
3. # Use lambda function with `filter()`
4. filtered_list = list(filter(lambda x: (x*2 > 10), my_list))
5. # Use lambda function with `map()`
6. mapped_list = list(map(lambda x: x*2, my_list))
7. # Use lambda function with `reduce()`
8. reduced_list = reduce(lambda x, y: x+y, my_list)
9.   print(filtered_list)
10.   print(mapped_list)
11.   print(reduced_list)

As the name states the filter() function it help filters the original list of inputs my_list based on a criterion > 10.By contrast, with map(), you implement a function to every components in the my_listlist. You multiply all of the components with two in this scenario. Remember that the function reduce() is a portion of the functools library. You cumulatively are using this function to the components in the my_list() list, from left to right, and in this situation decrease the sequence to a single value 55.

Using main() as a Function

If you have got any knowledge with other programming languages like java, you'll notice that executing functions requires the main feature. As you've known in the above examples, Python doesn't really require this. However, it can be helpful to logically organize your code along with a main() function in your python code- - all of the most important components are contained within this main() function.

You could even simply achieve and call a main() function the same as you did with all of those above functions:

1. # Define `main()` function

2. def main():

3. hello()

4. print("This is the main function")

5. main()

After all, as it now appears, when you load it as a module, the script of your main ( ) function will indeed be called. You invoke the main() function whenever name == ' main ' to ensure this does not happen.

That implies the source above code script becomes:

1.# Define `main()` function

2.def main():

3.hello()

4.print("This is a main function")

5.# Execute `main()` function

6. if __name__ == '__main__':

7. main()

Remember that in addition to the main function, you too have a init function, which validates a class or object instance. Plainly defined, it operates as a constructor or initializer, and is termed automatically when you start a new class instance. With such a function, the freshly formed object is assigned to the self-parameter that you've seen in this guide earlier.

Consider the following example:

class Dog:

    """

    Requires:

legs – legs for a dog to walk.

color – Fur color.

```python
"""

def __init__(self, legs, color):
self.legs = legs
self.color = color
def bark(self):
bark = "bark" * 2
return bark
if __name__ == "__main__":
dog = Dog(4, "brown")
bark = dog.bark()
print(bark)
```

LISTS AND LOOPS

Lists

A list is often a data structure in Python, which is an ordered list of elements that is mutable or modifiable. An item is named for each element or value inside a list. Just like strings are defined like characters between quotations, lists are specified by square brackets '[ ]' having values.

Lists are nice to have because you have other similar principles to deal with. They help you to hold data that are relevant intact, compress the code, and run the same numerous-value methods and processes at once.

It could be helpful to get all the several lists you have on your computer when beginning to think about Python lists as well as other data structures that are types of collections: Your assemblage of files, song playlists, browser bookmarks, emails, video collections that you can access through a streaming platform and much more.

We must function with this data table, taken from data collection of the Mobile App Store (RamanathanPerumal):

Name	price	currency	rating_count	rating
Instagram	0.0	USD	2161558	4.5

Clash of Clans	0.0	USD	2130805	4.5
Temple Run	0.0	USD	1724546	4.5
Pandora – Music & Radio	0.0	USD	1126879	4.0
Facebook	0.0	USD	2974676	3.5

Every value is a data point in the table. The first row (just after titles of the columns) for example has 5 data points:

Facebook

0.0

USD

2974676

3.5

Dataset consists of a collection of data points. We can consider the above table as a list of data points. Therefore we consider the entire list a dataset. We can see there are five rows and five columns to our data set.

Utilizing our insight of the Python types, we could perhaps consider we can store each data point in their own variable — for example, here's how we can store the data points of the first row:

```
script.py
track_name_row1 = 'Facebook'
price_row1 = 0.0
currency_row1 = 'USD'
rating_count_tot_row1 = 2974676
user_rating_row1 = 3.5
```

Above, we stored:

Text for the string as "Facebook."

Float 0.0 as a price

Text for the string as "USD."

Integer 2,974,676 as a rating count

Float 3.5 for user rating

A complicated process would be to create a variable for every data point in our data set. Luckily we can use lists to store data more effectively. So in the first row, we can draw up a list of data points:

```
script.py
row_1 = ['Facebook', 0.0, 'USD', 2974676, 3.5]
print(row_1)
type(row_1)

Output
['Facebook', 0.0, 'USD', 2974676, 3.5]
list
```

For list creation, we:

Separating each with a comma while typing out a sequence of data points: 'Facebook,' 0.0, 'USD,' 2974676, 3.5

Closing the list with square brackets: ['Facebook', 0.0, 'USD', 2974676, 3.5]

After the list is created, we assign it to a variable named row_1and the list is stored in the computer's memory.

For creating data points list, we only need to:

Add comma to the data points for separation.

Closing the list with brackets.

See below as we create five lists, in the dataset each row with one list:

```
row_1 =]['FACEBOOK', 0.0, 'usd', 2974676, 3.5]

row_2 = ['INSTAGRAM', 0.0, 'usd', 2161558, 4.5]

row_3 = ['CLASH OF CLANS', 0.0, 'usd', 2130805, 4.5]

row_4 = ['TEMPLE RUN', 0.0, 'usd', 1724546, 4.5]

row_5 =['PANDORA', 0.0, 'usd', 1126879, 4.0]
```

Index of Python Lists

A list could include a broader array of data types. A list containing [4, 5, 6] includes the same types of data (only integers), while the list ['Facebook', 0.0, 'USD,' 2974676, 3.5]

contains many types of data:

Consisting Two types of floats (0.0, 3.5)

Consisting One type of integer (2974676)

Consisting two types of strings ('Facebook,' 'USD')

['FACEBOOK', 0.0, 'usd', 2974676, 3.5] list got 5 data

points. For the length of a list, len() command can be used:

```
script.py
row_1 = ['Facebook', 0.0, 'USD', 2974676, 3.5]
print(len(row_1))

list_1 = [1, 6, 0]
print(len(list_1))

list_2 = []
print(len(list_2))

Output
5
3
0
```

For smaller lists, we can simply count the data points on our

displays to figure the length, but perhaps the len() command will

claim to be very useful anytime you function with lists containing

many components, or just need to compose data code where

you really don't know the length in advance.

Every other component (data point) in a list is linked to a

particular number, termed the index number. The indexing also begins at 0, which means that the first element should have the index number 0, the 2nd element the index number 1, etc.

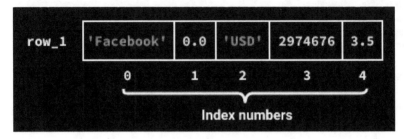

To locate a list element index rapidly, determine its location number in the list and then subtract it by 1. The string 'USD,' for instance, is the third item in the list (stance number 3), well its index number must be two because 3 − 1 = 2.

The index numbers enable us to locate a single item from a list. Going backward through the list row 1 from the example above, by executing code row 1[0], we can obtain the first node (the string 'Facebook') of index number 0.

```
script.py
row_1 = ['Facebook', 0.0, 'USD', 2974676, 3.5]
row_1[0]

Output
'Facebook'
```

The Model list_name[index number] follows the syntax for locating specific list components. For example, the title of our list above is row_1 and the index number of a first element is 0, we get row_1[0] continuing to follow the list_name[index number] model, in which the index number 0 is in square brackets just after the name of the variable row_1.

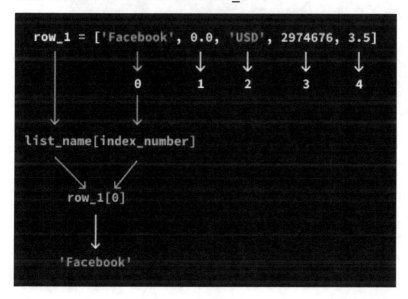

The method to retrieve each element in row_1:

```
script.py

row_1 = ['Facebook', 0.0, 'USD', 2974676, 3.5]
              0        1     2       3       4
              └─────────┘└────────────────────┘
                      Index numbers

print(row_1[0])
print(row_1[1])
print(row_1[2])
print(row_1[3])
print(row_1[4])
```
```
Output
Facebook
0.0
USD
2974676
3.5
```

Retrieval of list elements makes processes easier to execute. For example, Facebook and Instagram ratings can be selected, and the aggregate or distinction between the two can be found:

```
script.py
row_1 = ['Facebook', 0.0, 'USD', 2974676, 3.5]
row_2 = ['Instagram', 0.0, 'USD', 2161558, 4.5]

difference = row_2[4] - row_1[4]
average_rating = (row_1[4] + row_2[4]) / 2

print(difference)
print(average_rating)

Output
1.0
4.0
```

Try Using list indexing to retrieve and then average the number

of ratings with the first 3 rows:

ratings_1 = row_1[3]

ratings_2 = row_2[3]

ratings_3 = row_3[3]

total = ratings_1 + ratings_2 + ratings_3

average = total / 3

print(average)

2422346.3333333335

Using Negative Indexing with Lists

There are two indexing systems for lists in Python:

Positive indexing: The index number of the first element is 0; the index number of the second element is 1 and furthermore.

Negative indexing: The index number of the last element is -1; the index number of the second element is -2 and furthermore.

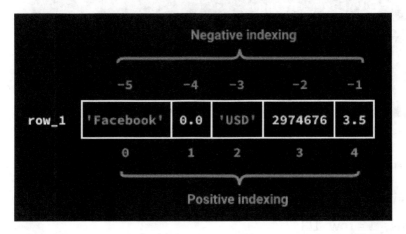

In exercise, we mostly use positive indexing to obtain elements of the list. Negative indexing is helpful whenever we want to pick the last element in such a list, mostly if the list is lengthy, and by calculating, we cannot figure out the length.

```
script.py
row_1 = ['Facebook', 0.0, 'USD', 2974676, 3.5]

print(row_1[-1])
print(row_1[4])

Output
3.5
3.5
```

Note that when we use an index number just outside of the scope of the two indexing schemes, we are going to have an IndexError.

```
script.py
row_1 = ['Facebook', 0.0, 'USD', 2974676, 3.5]
row_1[6]

Output
IndexError: list index out of range
```

```
script.py
row_1 = ['Facebook', 0.0, 'USD', 2974676, 3.5]
row_1[-7]

Output
IndexError: list index out of range
```

How about using negative indexing to remove from each of the top 3 rows the user rating (the very last value) and afterwards average it.

row_1 [-1]=rating_1

row_2[-1]=rating_2

row_3[-1]=rating_3

rating_1 + rating_2 + rating_3=total_rating

total_rating / 3= average_rating

print(average)

2422346.33333

Slice Python Lists

Rather than selecting the list elements separately, we can pick two consecutive elements using a syntax shortcut:

```
script.py
row_3 = ['Clash of Clans', 0.0, 'USD', 2130805, 4.5]

cc_pricing_data = row_3[0:3]  ⟵ syntax shortcut
print(cc_pricing_data)

Output
['Clash of Clans', 0.0, 'USD']
```

While selecting the first n elements from a list called a list (n stands for a number), we can use the list syntax shortcut [0: n]. In the above example, we had to choose from the list row 3 the first three elements, so we will use row 3[0:3].

When the first three items were chosen, we sliced a portion of the set. For this function, the collection method for a section of a list is known as list slicing.

List slice can be done in many ways:

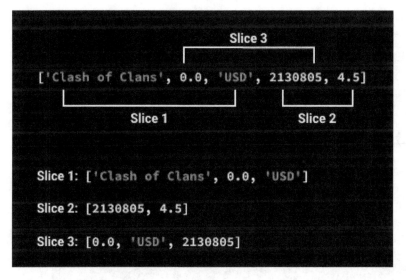

Retrieving any list slice we need:

Firstly identify the first and last elements of the slice.

The index numbers of the first and last element of the slice must then be defined.

Lastly, we can use the syntax a list[m: n] to extract the list slice we require, while:

'm' means the index number of both the slice's 1st element; and

'n' symbolizes the index number of the slice's last element in addition to one (if the last element seems to have index number 2, after which n is 3, if the last element seems to have index number 4, after which n is 5, and so on).

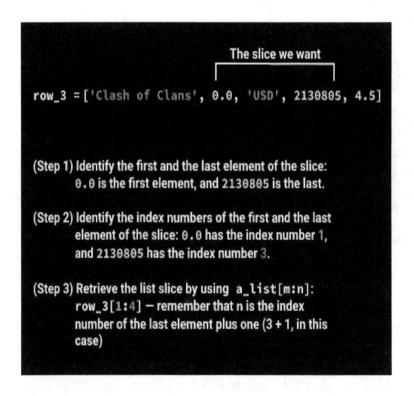

When we want to choose the 1st or last 'x' elements (x represents a number), we may use even less complex shortcuts for syntax:

a_list[:x] when we need to choose the first x elements.

a_list[-x:] when we need to choose the last x elements.

```
script.py
row_3 = ['Clash of Clans', 0.0, 'USD', 2130805, 4.5]

first_3 = row_3[:3]
last_3 = row_3[-3:]

print(first_3)
print(last_3)
```

```
Output
['Clash of Clans', 0.0, 'USD']
['USD', 2130805, 4.5]
```

See how we retrieve from the first row the first four elements (with Facebook data):

first_4_fb = row_1[:4]

print(first_4_fb)

['Facebook', 0.0, 'USD', 2974676]

From the same row, the last three elements are:

last_3_fb = row_1[-3:]

print(last_3_fb)

['USD', 2974676, 3.5]

In the fifth row (data in the row for Pandora) with elements third and fourth are:

```
pandora_3_4 = row_5[2:4]
print(pandora_3_4)
['USD', 1126879]
```

Python List of Lists

Lists were previously introduced as a viable approach to using one variable per data point. Rather than having a different variable for any of the five 'Facebook' data points, 0.0, 'USD,' 2974676, 3.5, we can connect the data points into a list together and then save the list in a variable.

We have worked with a data set of five rows since then and have stored each row as a collection in each different variable (row 1, row 2, row 3, row 4, and row 5 variables). Even so, if we had a data set of 5,000 rows, we would probably have ended up with 5,000 variables that will create our code messy and nearly difficult to work with.

To fix this issue, we may store our five variables in a unified list:

```
script.py
row_1 = ['Facebook', 0.0, 'USD', 2974676, 3.5]
row_2 = ['Instagram', 0.0, 'USD', 2161558, 4.5]
row_3 = ['Clash of Clans', 0.0, 'USD', 2130805, 4.5]
row_4 = ['Temple Run', 0.0, 'USD', 1724546, 4.5]
row_5 = ['Pandora - Music & Radio', 0.0, 'USD', 1126879, 4.0]

data_set = [row_1, row_2, row_3, row_4, row_5]
data_set
```

Output ———Notice the double brackets

```
[['Facebook', 0.0, 'USD', 2974676, 3.5],←——→ Notice the commas
['Instagram', 0.0, 'USD', 2161558, 4.5],←
['Clash of Clans', 0.0, 'USD', 2130805, 4.5],
['Temple Run', 0.0, 'USD', 1724546, 4.5],
['Pandora - Music & Radio', 0.0, 'USD', 1126879, 4.0]]
```

As we're seeing, the data set is a list of five additional columns
(row 1, row 2, row 3, row 4, and row 5). A list containing other
lists is termed a set of lists.

The data set variable is already a list, which indicates that we can
use the syntax we have learned to retrieve individual list
elements and execute list slicing. Under, we have:

Use datset[0] to locate the first list element (row 1).

Use datset[-1] to locate the last list element (row 5).

Obtain the first two list elements (row 1 and row 2) utilizing data
set[:2] to execute a list slicing.

```
script.py
data_set = [row_1, row_2, row_3, row_4, row_5]
print(data_set[0])
print(data_set[-1])
print(data_set[:2])

Output

['Facebook', 0.0, 'USD', 2974676, 3.5]
['Pandora - Music & Radio', 0.0, 'USD', 1126879, 4.0]
[['Facebook', 0.0, 'USD', 2974676, 3.5],
['Instagram', 0.0, 'USD', 2161558, 4.5]]
```

Often, we will need to obtain individual elements from a list that
is a portion of a list of lists — for example; we might need to
obtain the rating of 3.5 from the data row ['FACEBOOK', 0.0,
'USD', 2974676, 3.5], which is a portion of the list of data sets.
We retrieve 3.5 from data set below utilizing what we have
learnt:

Using data set[0], we locate row_1, and allocate the output to a
variable named fb_row.

fb_row ['Facebook', 0.0, 'USD', 2974676, 3.5] outputs, which we
printed.

Using fb_row[-1], we locate the final element from fb_row
(because fb row is a list), and appoint the output to a variable
called fb_rating.

Print fb_rating, outputting 3.5

```
script.py
data_set = [row_1, row_2, row_3, row_4, row_5]
fb_row = data_set[0]
print(fb_row)

fb_rating = fb_row[-1]
print(fb_rating)
```
```
Output
['Facebook', 0.0, 'USD', 2974676, 3.5]
3.5
```

Earlier in this example, we obtained 3.5 in two steps: data_set[0] was first retrieved, and fb_row[-1] was then retrieved. There is also an easy way to get the same 3.5 output by attaching the two indices ([0] and [-1]); the code data_set[0][-1] gets 3.5.:

```
script.py
data_set = [row_1, row_2, row_3, row_4, row_5]
print(data_set[0][-1])
           ⌣‾‾‾‾‾‾‾⌣
              row_1
              ⌣‾‾⌣
                ⊤
   ['Facebook', 0.0, 'USD', 2974676, 3.5]
```
```
Output
3.5
```

Earlier in this example, we have seen two ways to get the 3.5 value back. Both methods lead to the same performance (3.5), but the second approach requires fewer coding, as the steps we see from the example are elegantly integrated. As you can select an alternative, people generally prefer the latter.

Let's turn our five independent lists in to the list of lists:

app_data_set = [row_1, row_2, row_3, row_4, row_5]

then use:

print(app_data_set)

```
[
 ['FACEBOOK', 0.0, 'usd', 2974676, 3.5]

 ['INSTAGRAM', 0.0, 'usd', 2161558, 4.5

 ['CLASH OF CLANS', 0.0, 'usd', 2130805, 4.5]

 ['TEMPLE RUN', 0.0, 'usd', 1724546, 4.5]

 ['PANDORA', 0.0, 'usd', 1126879, 4.0]                    ]
```

List Processes by Repetitive method

Earlier, we had an interest in measuring an app's average ranking in this project. It was a feasible task while we were attempting to work only for three rows, but the tougher it becomes, the further rows we add. Utilizing our tactic from the beginning, we will:

Obtain each individual rating.

Take the sum of the ratings.

Dividing by the total number of ratings.

```
script.py
row_1 = ['Facebook', 0.0, 'USD', 2974676, 3.5]
row_2 = ['Instagram', 0.0, 'USD', 2161558, 4.5]
row_3 = ['Clash of Clans', 0.0, 'USD', 2130805, 4.5]
row_4 = ['Temple Run', 0.0, 'USD', 1724546, 4.5]
row_5 = ['Pandora - Music & Radio', 0.0, 'USD', 1126879, 4.0]

app_data_set = [row_1, row_2, row_3, row_4, row_5]
avg_rating = (app_data_set[0][-1] + app_data_set[1][-1] +
              app_data_set[2][-1] + app_data_set[3][-1] +
              app_data_set[4][-1]) / 5

avg_rating
```

```
Output
4.2
```

As you have seen that it becomes complicated with five ratings. Unless we were dealing with data that includes thousands of rows, an unimaginable amount of code would be needed! We ought to find a quick way to get lots of ratings back.

Taking a look at the code example earlier in this thread, we see that a procedure continues to reiterate: within app_data_set, we select the last list element for every list. What if we can just directly ask Python we would like to repeat this process in app_data_set for every list?

Luckily we can use it — Python gives us a simple route to repeat a plan that helps us tremendously when we have to reiterate a process tens of thousands or even millions of times.

Let's assume we have a list [3, 5, 1, 2] allocated to a variable rating, and we need to replicate the following procedure: display the element for each element in the ratings. And this is how we can turn it into syntax with Python:

```
script.py
ratings = [3, 5, 1, 2]

for element in ratings:
    print(element)
```

```
Output
3
5
1
2
```

The procedure that we decided to replicate in our first example above was "generate the last item for each list in the app_data_set." Here's how we can transform that operation into syntax with Python:

```
script.py
app_data_set = [row_1, row_2, row_3, row_4, row_5]

for each_list in app_data_set:
    rating = each_list[-1]
    print(rating)
```

```
Output
3.5
4.5
4.5
4.5
4.0
```

Let's attempt and then get a good idea of what's going on above. Python differentiates each list item from app_data_set, each at a time, and assign it to each_list (which essentially becomes a vector that holds a list — we'll address this further):

```
script.py

app_data_set = [row_1, row_2, row_3, row_4, row_5]

for each_list in app_data_set:
    print(each_list)
```

```
Output

['Facebook', 0.0, 'USD', 2974676, 3.5]
['Instagram', 0.0, 'USD', 2161558, 4.5]
['Clash of Clans', 0.0, 'USD', 2130805, 4.5]
['Temple Run', 0.0, 'USD', 1724546, 4.5]
['Pandora - Music & Radio', 0.0, 'USD', 1126879, 4.0]
```

In the last figure earlier in this thread, the code is a much simpler and much more conceptual edition of the code below:

```
script.py

app_data_set = [row_1, row_2, row_3, row_4, row_5]

print(app_data_set[0])  ⎫
print(app_data_set[1])  ⎪
print(app_data_set[2])  ⎬  for each_list in app_data_set:
print(app_data_set[3])  ⎪       print(each_list)
print(app_data_set[4])  ⎭
```

```
Output

['Facebook', 0.0, 'USD', 2974676, 3.5]
['Instagram', 0.0, 'USD', 2161558, 4.5]
['Clash of Clans', 0.0, 'USD', 2130805, 4.5]
['Temple Run', 0.0, 'USD', 1724546, 4.5]
['Pandora - Music & Radio', 0.0, 'USD', 1126879, 4.0]
```

Utilizing the above technique requires that we consider writing a line of code for each row in the data set. But by using the app_data_set methodology for each list involves that we write only two lines of code irrespective of the number of rows in the data set — the data set may have five rows or a hundred thousand.

Our transitional goal is to use this special method to calculate the average rating of our five rows above, in which our ultimate goal is to calculate the average rating of 7,197 rows for our data set. We 're going to get exactly that within the next few displays of this task, but we're going to concentrate for now on practicing this method to get a strong grasp of it.

We ought to indent the space characters four times to the right before we want to write the code:

```
script.py

app_data_set = [row_1, row_2, row_3, row_4, row_5]

for each_list in app_data_set:
    print(each_list)
```

We need to indent the code we want repeated
four space characters to the right

Theoretically, we would only have to indent the code to the right with at least one space character, but in the Python language, the declaration is to use four space characters. This assists with readability — reading your code will be fairly easy for other individuals who watch this convention, and you will find it easier to follow theirs.

Now use this technique to print each app's name and rating:

```
foreach_list in app_data_set:
name = each_list[0]
rating = each_list[-1]
print(name, rating)
```

Facebook 3.5

Instagram 4.5

Clash of Clans 4.5

Temple Run 4.5

Pandora - Music & Radio 4.0

Loops

A loop is frequently used to iterate over a series of statements. We have two kinds of loops, 'for loop' and 'while loop' in Python. We will study 'for loop' and 'while loop' in the following scenario.

For Loop

Python's for loop is used to iterate over a sequence (list, tuple, string) or just about any iterate-able object. It is called traversal to iterate over a sequence.

Syntax of For loop in Python

for<variable> in <sequence>:

   # body_of_loop that has set of statements

   # which requires repeated execution

In this case < variable > is often a variable used to iterate over a < sequence >. Around each iteration the next value is taken from < sequence > to approach the end of the sequence.

Python – For loop example

The example below illustrates the use of a loop to iterate over a list array. We calculate the square of each number present in the list and show the same with the body of for loop.

```
#Printing squares of all numbers program
# List of integer numbers
numbers = [1, 2, 4, 6, 11, 20]
#variable to store each number's square temporary
sq = 0
#iterating over the given list
forval in numbers:
    # calculating square of each number
sq = val * val
```

    # displaying the squares

print(sq)

Output:

1

4

16

36

121

400

For loop with else block

Excluding Java, we can have the loop linked with an optional 'else' block in Python. The 'else' block only runs after all the iterations are finished by the loop. Let's see one example:

For val in range(5):

    print(val)

else:

    print("The loop has completed execution")

Output:

0

1

2

3

4

The loop has completed execution

Note: else block is executed when the loop is completed.

Nested For loop in Python

If there is a loop within another for loop, then it will be termed a nested for loop. Let's take a nested for loop example.

```
for num1 in range(3):
        for num2 in range(10, 14):
                print(num1, ",", num2)
```

Output:

0 , 10

0 , 11

0 , 12

0 , 13

1 , 10

1 , 11

1 , 12

1 , 13

2 , 10

2 , 11

2 , 12

2 , 13

While Loop

While loop is also used to continuously iterate over a block of code until a specified statement returns false, we have seen in many for loop in Python in the last guide, which is used for a similar intent. The biggest distinction is that we use for looping when we are not sure how many times the loop needs execution, yet on the other side when we realize exactly how many times we have to execute the loop, we need for a loop. Syntax of while loop

while conditioning:

```
#body_of_while
```

The body of the while is a series of statements from Python which require repetitive implementation. These claims are consistently executed until the specified condition returns false.

while loop flow

1. Firstly given condition is inspected, the loop is canceled if the condition returns false, and also the control moves towards the next statement in the compiler after the loop.

2. When the condition returns true, the set of statements within the loop will be performed, and the power will then switch to the loop start for the next execution.

Those two measures continuously occur as long as the condition defined in the loop stands true.

While loop example

This is an example of a while loop. We have a variable number in this case, and we show the value of the number in a loop, the loop will have an incremental operation where we increase the number value. It is a very crucial component, while the loop should have an operation of increase or decrease. Otherwise, the loop will operate indefinitely.

num = 1

#loop will repeat itself as long as it can

#num< 10 remains true

whilenum< 10:`

print(num)

   #incrementing the value of num

num = num + 3

Output:

1

4

Infinite while loop

Example 1:

This will endlessly print the word 'hello' since this situation will always be true.

```
while True:
print("hello")
```

Example 2:

```
num = 1
whilenum<5:
print(num)
```

This will endlessly print '1' since we do not update the number value inside the loop, so the number value would always remain one, and the condition number<5 would always give back true.

Nested while loop in Python

While inside another while loop a while loop is present, then it will be considered nested while loop. To understand this concept, let us take an example.

```
i = 1
j = 5
while i< 4:
```

```
while j < 8:
print(i, ",", j)
    j = j + 1
i = i + 1
```

Output:

```
1 , 5
2 , 6
3 , 7
```

Python – while loop with else block

We may add an 'else' block to a while loop. The section 'else' is possible. It executes only when the processing of the loop has ended.

```
num = 10
whilenum> 6:
print(num)
num = num-1
else:
print("loop is finished")
```

Output:

```
10
9
8
```

7

Loop is finished

ADDING MULTIPLE VALUED DATA IN PYTHON

Often the creator wants users to input multiple values or inputs in a line. In Python, users could use two techniques to take multiple values or inputs in one line.

Use of split() method

Use of List comprehension

Use of split() method :

This feature helps to receive many user inputs. It splits the defined separator to the given input. If no separator is given, then a separator is blank space. Users generally use a split() method to separate a Python string, but it can be used when multiple inputs are taken.

Syntax:

input().split(separator, maxsplit)

Example:

```
filter_none
edit
play_arrow
brightness_4
#Python program showing how to add
#multiple input using split
#taking two inputs each time
x, y = input("Enter a two value: ").split()
print("Number of boys: ", x)
print("Number of girls: ", y)
print()
# taking three inputs at a time
x, y, z = input("Enter a three value: ").split()
print("Total number of students: ", x)
print("Number of boys is : ", y)
print("Number of girls is : ", z)
print()
# taking two inputs at a time
a, b = input("Enter a two value: ").split()
print("First number is {} and second number is {}".format(a, b))
print()
# taking multiple inputs at a time
# and type casting using list() function
x = list(map(int, input("Enter a multiple value: ").split()))
print("List of students: ", x)
```

Output:

```
Enter a two value: 5 10
Number of boys:   5
Number of girls:   10

Enter a three value: 30 10 20
Total number of students:   30
Number of boys is :   10
Number of girls is :   20

Enter a four value: 20 30
First number is 20 and second number is 30

Enter a multiple value: 20 30 10 22 23 26
List of students:   [20, 30, 10, 22, 23, 26]
```

Using List comprehension:

Comprehension of lists is an easy way of describing and building a list in Python. Just like mathematical statements, we can generate lists within each line only. It is often used when collecting multiple device inputs.

Example:

```
filter_none
edit
play_arrow
brightness_4
# Python program showing
# how to take multiple input
# using List comprehension
# taking two input at a time
x, y = [int(x) for x in input("Enter two value: ").split()]
print("First Number is: ", x)
print("Second Number is: ", y)
print()
# taking three input at a time
x, y, z = [int(x) for x in input("Enter three value: ").split()]
print("First Number is: ", x)
print("Second Number is: ", y)
print("Third Number is: ", z)
print()
# taking two inputs at a time
x, y = [int(x) for x in input("Enter two value: ").split()]
print("First number is {} and second number is {}".format(x, y))
print()
# taking multiple inputs at a time
x = [int(x) for x in input("Enter multiple value: ").split()]
print("Number of list is: ", x)
```

Output:

```
Enter two value: 2 5
First Number is:   2
Second Number is:   5

Enter three value: 2 4 5
First Number is:   2
Second Number is:   4
Third Number is:   5

Enter two value: 2 10
First number is 2 and second number is 10

Enter multiple value: 1 2 3 4 5
Number of list is:   [1, 2, 3, 4, 5]
```

Note: The definitions above take inputs divided by spaces. If we prefer to pursue different input by comma (","), we can just use the below:

```
# taking multiple inputs divided by comma at a time
x = [int(x) for x in input("Enter multiple value: ").split(",")]
print("Number of list is: ", x)
```

Assign multiple values to multiple variables

By separating the variables and values with commas, you can allocate multiple values to different variables.

```
a, b = 100, 200
print(a)
# 100
print(b)
# 200
```

You have more than three variables to delegate. In addition, various types can be assigned, as well.

```
a, b, c = 0.1, 100, 'string'
print(a)
# 0.1
print(b)
# 100
print(c)
#string
```

Assign the same value to multiple variables

Using = consecutively, you could even appoint multiple variables with the same value. For instance, this is helpful when you initialize multiple variables to almost the same value.

```
a = b = 100
print(a)
# 100
print(b)
# 100
```

Upon defining the same value, another value may also be converted into one. As explained later, when allocating mutable objects such as lists or dictionaries, care should be taken.

```
a = 200
print(a)
```

```
# 200

print(b)

# 100
```

It can be written three or more in the same way.

```
a = b = c = 'string'

print(a)

# string

print(b)

# string

print(c)

# string
```

Instead of immutable objects like int, float, and str, be careful when appointing mutable objects like list and dict.

When you use = consecutively, all variables are assigned the same object, so if you modify the element value or create a new element, then the other object will also modify.

```
a = b = [0, 1, 2]

print(a is b)

# True

a[0] = 100

print(a)

# [100, 1, 2]

print(b)

# [100, 1, 2]
```

Same as below.

```
b = [0, 1, 2]
a = b
print(a is b)
# True
a[0] = 100
print(a)
# [100, 1, 2]
print(b)
# [100, 1, 2]
```

If you would like to independently manage them you need to allocate them separately.

after c = []; d = [], c and d are guaranteed to link to two unique, newly created empty,different lists. (Note that c = d = [] assigns the same object to both c and d.)

Here is another example:

```
a = [0, 1, 2]
b = [0, 1, 2]
print(a is b)
# False
a[0] = 100
print(a)
# [100, 1, 2]
print(b)
```

[0, 1, 2]

Adding string data in Python

What is String in Python?

A string is a Character set. A character is just a symbol. The English language, for instance, has 26 characters. Operating systems do not handle characters they handle the (binary) numbers. And if you may see characters on your computer, it is represented internally as a mixture of 0s and 1s and is manipulated. The transformation of character to a number is known as encoding, and probably decoding is the reverse process. ASCII and Unicode are two of the widely used encodings. A string in Python is a series of characters in Unicode. Unicode was incorporated to provide all characters in all languages and to carry encoding uniformity. Python Unicode allows you to learn regarding Unicode.

How to create a string in Python?

Strings may be formed by encapsulating characters or even double quotes inside a single quotation. In Python, even triple quotes may be used but commonly used to portray multiline strings and docstrings.

```python
# defining strings in Python

# all of the following are equivalent

my_string = 'Hello'

print(my_string)

my_string = "Hello"

print(my_string)

my_string = '''Hello'''

print(my_string)

# triple quotes string can extend multiple lines

my_string = """Hello, welcome to the world of Python"""

print(my_string)
```

When the program is executed, the output becomes:

```
Hello

Hello

Hello

Hello, welcome to the world of Python
```

Accessing the characters in a string?

By indexing and using slicing, we can obtain individual characters and scope of characters. The index commences at 0. Attempting to obtain a character from index range will cause an IndexError to increase. The index has to be integral. We cannot use floats or other types, and this will lead to TypeError. Python lets its sequences be indexed negatively. The -1 index corresponds to the last object, -2 to the second object, and so forth. Using the slicing operator '(colon),' we can access a range of items within a string.

#Python string characters access:

```
str = 'programiz'
print('str = ', str)
#first character
print('str[0] = ', str[0])
#last character
print('str[-1] = ', str[-1])
#slicing 2nd to 5th character
print('str[1:5] = ', str[1:5])
#slicing 6th to 2nd last character
print('str[5:-2] = ', str[5:-2])
```

If we execute the code above we have the following results:

```
str =  programiz
str[0] =  p
str[-1] =  z
str[1:5] =  rogr
str[5:-2] =  am
```

When we attempt to access an index out of the range, or if we are using numbers other than an integer, errors will arise.

index must be in the range

```
>>>my_string[15]

...

IndexError: string index out of range

# index must be an integer

>>>my_string[1.5]

...
```

TypeError: Define string indices as integers only

By analyzing the index between the elements as seen below, slicing can best be visualized. Whenever we want to obtain a range, we need the index that slices the part of the string from it.

How to change or delete a string?

Strings are unchangeable. This means elements of a list cannot be modified until allocated. We will easily reassign various strings of the same term.

```
>>>my_string = 'programiz'
>>>my_string[5] = 'a'
...
TypeError: 'str' object does not support item assignment
>>>my_string = 'Python'
>>>my_string
'Python'
```

We cannot erase characters from a string, or remove them. But it's easy to erase the string completely by using del keyword.

```
>>>delmy_string[1]
...
TypeError: 'str' object doesn't support item deletion
>>>delmy_string
>>>my_string
...
NameError: name 'my_string' is not defined
```

Python String Operations

There are many methods that can be used with string making it one of the most commonly used Python data types. See Python Data Types for more information on the types of data used in Python coding

Concatenation of Two or More Strings

The combination of two or even more strings into one is termed concatenation. In Python, the + operator does that. They are likewise concatenated by actually typing two string literals together. For a specified number of times, the * operator could be used to reiterate the string.

```
# Python String Operations

str1 = 'Hello'

str2 ='World!'

# using +

print('str1 + str2 = ', str1 + str2)

# using *

print('str1 * 3 =', str1 * 3)
```

Once we execute the program above we get the following results:

str1 + str2 = HelloWorld!

str1 * 3 = HelloHelloHello

Using two literal strings together would therefore concatenate them like + operator.

We might use parentheses if we wish to concatenate strings in various lines.

```
>>> # two string literals together

>>> 'Hello ''World!'

'Hello World!'

>>> # using parentheses

>>> s = ('Hello '

...       'World')

>>>s

'Hello World'
```

Iterating Through a string

With a for loop, we can iterate through a string. This is an example of counting the number of 'l's in a string function.

```
#Iterating through a string

count = 0

for letter in 'Hello World':

if(letter == 'l'):

count += 1

print(count,'letters found')
```

If we execute the code above, we have the following results:
'3 letters found.'

String Membership Test

We can check whether or not there is a substring within a string
by using keyword in.

>>> 'a' in 'program'

True

>>> 'at' not in 'battle'

False

Built-in functions to Work with Python

Different built-in functions which can also be work with strings in
series. A few other commonly used types are len() and
enumerate(). The function enumerate() returns an enumerate
object. It includes the index and value as combinations of all

elements in the string. This may be of use to iteration.

Comparably, len() returns the string length (characters number).

```
str = 'cold'

# enumerate()

list_enumerate = list(enumerate(str))

print('list(enumerate(str) = ', list_enumerate)

#character count

print('len(str) = ', len(str))
```

Once we execute the code above we have the following results:

```
list(enumerate(str) =  [(0, 'c'), (1, 'o'), (2, 'l'), (3, 'd')]

len(str) =  4
```

Formats for Python String

Sequence for escaping

We can't use single quotes or double quotes if we want to print a text like He said, "What's there?" This would result in a SyntaxError because there are single and double quotations in the text alone.

```
>>>print("He said, "What's there?"")
...
```

SyntaxError: invalid syntax

```
>>>print('He said, "What's there?"')
...
```

SyntaxError: invalid syntax

Triple quotes are one way to get round the problem. We might use escape sequences as a solution. A series of escape starts with a backslash, which is represented differently. If we are using a single quote to describe a string, it is important to escape all single quotes within the string. The case with double quotes is closely related. This is how the above text can be represented.

```
# using triple quotes
print('''He said, "What's there?"''')
# escaping single quotes
print('He said, "What\'s there?"')
# escaping double quotes
print("He said, \"What's there?\"")
```

Once we execute the code above, we have the following results:

He said, "What's there?"
He said, "What's there?"
He said, "What's there?"

Raw String to ignore escape sequence

Quite often inside a string, we might want to reject the escape sequences. To use it, we can set r or R before the string. Which

means it's a raw string, and it will neglect any escape sequence
inside.

>>>print("This is \x61 \ngood example")

This is a

good example

>>> print(r"This is \x61 \ngood example")

This is \x61 \ngood example

The format() Method for Formatting Strings

The format() sources available and make with the string object is
very flexible and potent in string formatting. Style strings contain
curly braces{} as placeholders or fields of substitution, which are
substituted.

To specify the sequence, we may use positional arguments or
keyword arguments.

```
# Python string format() method
# default(implicit) order
default_order = "{}, {} and {}".format('John','Bill','Sean')
print('\n--- Default Order ---')
print(default_order)
# order using positional argument
positional_order = "{1}, {0} and {2}".format('John','Bill','Sean')
print('\n--- Positional Order ---')
print(positional_order)
# order using keyword argument
keyword_order = "{s}, {b} and {j}".format(j='John',b='Bill',s='Sean')
print('\n--- Keyword Order ---')
print(keyword_order)
Once we execute the code above we have the following results:
--- Default Order ---
John, Bill and Sean
--- Positional Order ---
Bill, John and Sean
--- Keyword Order ---
Sean, Bill and John
```

The format() technique can have requirements in optional format. Using colon, they are divided from the name of the field. For example, a string in the given space may be left-justified <, right-justified >, or based ^.

Even we can format integers as binary, hexadecimal, etc. and floats can be rounded or shown in the style of the exponent. You can use tons of compiling there. For all string formatting available using the format() method, see below example:

```
>>> # formatting integers
>>> "Binary representation of {0} is {0:b}".format(12)
'Binary representation of 12 is 1100'
>>> # formatting floats
>>> "Exponent representation: {0:e}".format(1566.345)
'Exponent representation: 1.566345e+03'
>>> # round off
>>> "One third is: {0:.3f}".format(1/3)
'One third is: 0.333'
>>> # string alignment
>>> "|{:<10}|{:^10}|{:>10}|".format('butter','bread','ham')
'|butter    |   bread  |       ham|'
```

Old style formatting

We even can code strings such as the old sprint() style in the programming language used in C. To accomplish this; we use the '%' operator.

```
>>> x = 12.3456789

>>>print('The value of x is %3.2f' %x)

The value of x is 12.35

>>>print('The value of x is %3.4f' %x)

The value of x is 12.3457
```

String common Methods for Python

The string object comes with various methods. One of them is the format() method we described above. A few other frequently used technique include lower(), upper(), join(), split(), find(), substitute() etc. Here is a wide-range list of several of the built-in methodologies in Python for working with strings.

```
>>> "PrOgRaMiZ".lower()

'programiz'

>>> "PrOgRaMiZ".upper()

'PROGRAMIZ'

>>> "This will split all words into a list".split()

['This', 'will', 'split', 'all', 'words', 'into', 'a', 'list']

>>> ' '.join(['This', 'will', 'join', 'all', 'words', 'into', 'a', 'string'])

'This will join all words into a string'

>>> 'Happy New Year'.find('ew')

7

>>> 'Happy New Year'.replace('Happy','Brilliant')

'Brilliant New Year'
```

Inserting values into strings

Method 1 - the string format method

The string method format method can be used to create new strings with the values inserted. That method works for all of Python's recent releases. That is where we put a string in another string:

```
>>>shepherd = "Mary"

>>>string_in_string = "Shepherd {} is on duty.".format(shepherd)

>>>print(string_in_string)
```

Shepherd Mary is on duty.

The curved braces indicate where the inserted value will be going.

You can insert a value greater than one. The values should not have to be strings; numbers and other Python entities may be strings.

```
>>>shepherd = "Mary"
>>>age = 32
>>>stuff_in_string = "Shepherd {} is {} years old.".format(shepherd, age)
>>>print(stuff_in_string)
Shepherd Mary is 32 years old.
>>> 'Here is a {} floating point number'.format(3.33333)
'Here is a 3.33333 floating point number'
```

Using the formatting options within curly brackets, you can do more complex formatting of numbers and strings — see the information on curly brace string layout.

This process allows us to give instructions for formatting things such as numbers, using either: inside the curly braces, led by guidance for formatting. Here we request you to print in integer (d) in which the number is 0 to cover the field size of 3:

```
>>>print("Number {:03d} is here.".format(11))
Number 011 is here.
```

This prints a floating point value (f) with exactly 4 digits after the decimal point:

```
>>> 'A formatted number - {:.4f}'.format(.2)
'A formatted number - 0.2000'
```

Method 2 - f-strings in Python >= 3.6

When you can rely on having Python > = version 3.6, you will have another appealing place to use the new literal (f-string) formatted string to input variable values. Just at the start of the string, an f informs Python to permit any presently valid variable names inside the string as column names. So here's an example such as the one above, for instance using the f-string syntax:

```
>>>shepherd = "Martha"
>>>age = 34
>>> # Note f before first quote of string
>>>stuff_in_string = f"Shepherd {shepherd} is {age} years old."
>>>print(stuff_in_string)
```

Shepherd Martha is 34 years old.

Method 3 - old school % formatting

There seems to be an older string formatting tool, which uses the percent operator. It is a touch less versatile than the other two choices, but you can still see it in use in older coding, where it is more straightforward to use '%' formatting. For formatting the '%' operator, you demonstrate where the encoded values should go using a '%' character preceded by a format identifier to tell how to add the value.

So here's the example earlier in this thread, using formatting by '%.' Note that '%s' marker for a string to be inserted, and the '%d' marker for an integer.

```
>>>stuff_in_string = "Shepherd %s is %d years old." % (shepherd, ag
>>>print(stuff_in_string)
```

Shepherd Martha is 34 years old.

MODULE DATA

What are the modules in Python?

Whenever you leave and re-enter the Python interpreter, the definitions you have created (functions and variables) will get lost. Consequently, if you'd like to develop a code a little longer, it's better to use a text editor to plan the input for the interpreter and execute it with that file as input conversely. This is defined as script formation. As the software gets bigger, you may want to break it into different files to make maintenance simpler. You might also like to use a handy function that you wrote in many other programs without having to replicate its definition inside each program. To assist this, Python has the option of putting definitions into a file and using them in the interpreter's code or interactive instances. This very file is considered a module; module descriptions can be loaded into certain modules or into the main module (the list of variables you have exposure to in a high-level script and in converter mode).

A module is a file that contains definitions and statements from Python. The name of the file is the name of the module with the .py suffix attached. The name of the module (only as string) inside a module is available as the value, including its global variable __name__. For example, use your preferred text editor to build a file named fibo.py with the following contents in the current working directory:

```
# Python Module example

def add(a, b):

    """This program adds two

numbers and return the result"""

result = a + b

return result
```

In this, we defined an add() function within an example titled " module." The function requires two numbers and returns a total of them.

How to import modules in Python?

Within a module, we can import the definitions to some other module or even to the interactive Python interpreter. To do something like this, we use the keyword import. To load our recently specified example module, please enter in the Python prompt.

```
>>> import example
```

This should not import the identities of the functions directly in the existing symbol table, as defined in the example. It just imports an example of the module name there.

Using the name of the module, we can use the dot(.) operator to access the function. For instance:

>>>example.add(4,5.5)

9.5

Python comes with lots of regular modules. Check out the complete list of regular Python modules and their usage scenarios. These directories are within the destination where you've installed Python in the Lib directory. Normal modules could be imported just the same as our user-defined modules are imported.

There are different ways of importing the modules. You'll find them below:

Python import statement

Using the import statement, we can extract a module by using the dot operator, as explained in the previous section and access the definitions within it. Here is another example.

```
# import statement example

# to import standard module math

import math

print("The value of pi is", math.pi)
```

Once we execute the code above, we have the following results:
The value of pi is 3.141592653589793

Import with renaming

We can load a module in the following way by changing the name of it:

```
# import module by renaming it

import math as m

print("The value of pi is", m.pi)
```

We called the module Math as m. In certain instances, this will save us time to type. Remember that in our scope, the name math is not identified. Therefore math.pi is incorrect, and m.pi is correctly implemented.

Python from...import statement

We can import individual names from such a module without having to import the entire module. Here is another example.

```
# import only pi from math module

from math import pi

print("The value of pi is", pi)
```

In this, only the pi parameter was imported from the math module. We don't utilize the dot operator in certain cases. We can likewise import different modules:

>>>from math import pi, e

>>>pi

3.141592653589793

>>>e

2.718281828459045

Import all names

With the following form, we can import all terms (definitions) from a module:

import all names from standard module math

from math import *

print("The value of pi is," pi)

Above, we have added all of the math module descriptions. This covers all names that are available in our scope except those that start with an underscore. It is not a good programming technique to import something with the asterisk (*) key. This will lead to a replication of an attribute's meaning. This also restricts our code's readability.

Python Module Search Path

Python looks at many locations when importing a module. Interpreter searches for a built-in module instead. So if not included in the built-in module, Python searches at a collection of directories specified in sys.path. The exploration is in this sequence:

PYTHONPATH (list of directories environment variable)

The installation-dependent default directory

```
>>> import sys

>>>sys.path

['',

'C:\\Python33\\Lib\\idlelib',

'C:\\Windows\\system32\\python33.zip',

'C:\\Python33\\DLLs',

'C:\\Python33\\lib',

'C:\\Python33',

'C:\\Python33\\lib\\site-packages']
```

We can insert that list and customize it to insert our own location.

Reloading a module

During a session, the Python interpreter needs to import one module only once. This makes matters more productive. Here is an example showing how that operates.

Assume we get the code below in a module called my_module:

```
# This module shows the effect of

#  multiple imports and reload

print("This code got executed")
```

Now we suspect that multiple imports have an impact.

>>> import my_module

This code was executed:

>>> import my_module

>>> import my_module

We have seen our code was only executed once. This means that our module has only been imported once.

Also, if during the process of the test our module modified, we will have to restart it. The way to do so is to reload the interpreter. But that doesn't massively help. Python offers an effective way to do so. Within the imp module, we may use the reload() function to restart a module. Here are some ways to do it:

```
>>> import imp
>>> import my_module
This code executes
>>> import my_module
>>>imp.reload(my_module)
This code executes
<module 'my_module' from '.\\my_module.py'>
```

The dir() built-in function

We may use the dir() function to locate names specified within a module. For such cases, in the example of the module that we had in the early part, we described a function add().

In example module, we can use dir in the following scenario:

```
>>>dir(example)

['__builtins__',

'__cached__',

'__doc__',

'__file__',

'__initializing__',

'__loader__',

'__name__',

'__package__',

'add']
```

Now we'll see a list of the names sorted (alongside add). Many
other names that start with an underscore are module-
associated (not user-defined) default Python attributes. For
instance, the attribute name contains module __name__.
>>> import example
>>>example.__name__
'example'
You can find out all names identified in our existing namespace
by using dir() function with no arguments.

```
>>> a = 1

>>> b = "hello"

>>> import math

>>>dir()

['__name__', '__doc__','__builtins__ ', 'a', 'b', 'math', 'pyscripter']
```

Executing modules as scripts

Python module running with python fibo.py <arguments>the
program will be running in such a way, just like it was being
imported, but including the __name__ set to "__main__." That
implies this program is inserted at the end of the module:

If __name__ == "__main__": import sys fib(int(sys.argv[1]))

You could even create the file usable both as a script and as an
importable module since this code parsing the command - line
interface runs only when the module is performed as the "main"
file:

$ python fibo.py 50

0 1 1 2 3 5 8 13

When the module is imported, the code will not be executed:

>>>

>>> import fibo

>>>

It is most often used whether to get an efficient user interface to a module or for test purposes (the module runs a test suite as a script).

"Compiled" Python files

To speed up loading modules, Python caches the compiled version of each module in the __pycache__ directory with the name module.version.pyc, in which the version encapsulates the assembled file format; it normally includes the firmware version of Python. For instance, the compiled edition of spam.py in CPython launch 3.3 will be cached as __pycache__/spam.cpython-33.pyc. This naming convention enables the coexistence of compiled modules from various updates and separate versions of Python.

Python tests the source change schedule against the compiled edition to see if it is out-of-date and needs recompilation. That's a fully automated system. Even the assembled modules become platform-independent, so different algorithms will use the same library between systems. In two situations Pythoniswill not check the cache:

First, it often recompiles the output for the module, which is loaded explicitly from the command line but does not store it. Second, when there is no root module, it will not search the cache. The compiled module must be in the source directory to facilitate a non-source (compiled only) release, and a source module should not be installed.

Some tips for users:

To minimize the size of a compiled file, you can use the -O or -OO switches in the Python order. The -O switch erases statements of assert, the -OO switch removes statements of assert as well as strings of doc. Although some codes may support getting these options available, this method should only be used if you are aware of what you are doing. "Optimized" modules usually have such an opt-tag and are tinier. Future releases may modify the optimal control implications.

A project run no faster once it is read from a.pyc file than how it was read from a.py file; just one thing about.pyc files that are faster in the speed with which they will be loaded.

A compile all modules can generate .pyc files in a directory for all of the other modules.

More details on this process are given in PEP 3147, along with a flow chart of the decision making.

Standard Modules

Python has a standard modules library, mentioned in a separate section, the Python Library allusion (hereafter "Library Reference"). A few modules are incorporated into the interpreter; that provide direct exposure to processes that are not component of the language's base but are nonetheless built-in, whether for effectiveness or to supply access to primitive operating systems such as source code calls. The collection of these modules is an alternative to customize and also relies on the framework underlying it. The winreg module, for instance, is only available on Microsoft windows. One particular module is worthy of certain interest: sys, which is integrated into every Python interpreter. The sys.ps1 and sys.ps2 variables classify strings which are used as primary and secondary instructions:

```
>>>
>>> import sys
>>> sys.ps1
'>>> '
>>> sys.ps2
'... '
>>> sys.ps1 = 'C> '
C>print('Yuck!')
Yuck!
```

C>

Only when the interpreter is in interactive mode are those two variables defined. The sys.path variable is a collection of strings that defines the search path for modules used by the interpreter. When PYTHONPATH is not a part of the set, then it will be defined to a predefined path taken from either the PYTHONPATH environment variable or through a built-in default. You can change it with regular list procedures:

```
>>>
>>> import sys
>>>sys.path.append('/python/ufs/guido/lib/')
```

Packages

Packages are indeed a way to construct the namespace of the Python module by using "pointed names of the module." For instance, in a package called A., the module title A.B specifies a submodule named B. Even as the use of modules prevents the writers of various modules from stopping to know about the global variable names of one another, any use of dotted module names prevents the developers of multi-module bundles like NumPy or Pillow from needing to worry more about module names of one another. Consider making a series of lists of modules (a "package") to handle sound files and sound data in an even manner.

There are several various programs of sound files usually familiar with their extension, for example: 'wav,.aiff,.au,' though you'll need to build and maintain a massive collection of modules to convert between some of the multiple formats of files. There are several other different operations that you may like to run on sound data (such as blending, adding echo, implementing an equalizer function, producing an optical stereo effect), and you'll just be writing an infinite series of modules to execute those interventions. Here is another feasible package layout (described in terms of a hierarchical file system):

```
sound/                          Top level package
    __init__.py                 sound package initialization
formats/                        Subpackage for conversions of file format
            __init__.py
            wavread.py
            wavwrite.py
            aiffread.py
            aiffwrite.py
            auread.py
            auwrite.py
            ...
effects/                Sound effectssubpackage
            __init__.py
            echo.py
            surround.py
            reverse.py
            ...
filters/                    Filterssubpackage
            __init__.py
            equalizer.py
            vocoder.py
            karaoke.py
            ...
```

While loading the bundle, Python checks for the packet subdirectory via the folders on sys.path. To allow Python view directories that hold the file as packages, the __init__.py files are needed. This protects directories with a common name, including string, from accidentally hiding valid modules, which later appear mostly on the search path of the module. In the correct order; __init__.py can only be a blank file, but it could also implement the package preprocessing code or establish the variable __all__ described below

Package users could even upload individual modules from the package, such as: 'import sound.effects.echo'

This loads the 'sound.effects.echo' sub-module. Its full name must be mentioned: 'sound.effects.echo.echofilter(input, output, atten=4, delay=0.7)'

Another way to import the submodule is: 'fromsound.effects import echo'

It, therefore, launches the sub-module echo and provides access but without package prefix: 'echo.echofilter(input, output, atten=4, delay=0.7)'

And just another option is to explicitly import the desired function or attribute: 'fromsound.effects.echo import echofilter'

This again activates the echo sub-module however this enables its echofilter() feature explicitly accessible: 'echofilter(input, output, delay=0.7, atten=4)'

So it heaps the sub-module echo; however this tends to make its function; remember that the object will either be a sub-module (or sub-package)of the package or any other name described in the package, such as a function, class or variable while using from package import object. Initially, the import statement analyses if the object is characterized in the package; otherwise, it supposes that it is a module and makes an attempt to load it. Once it fails to reach it, an exception to 'ImportError' will be promoted.

Referring to this, while using syntax such as import 'item.subitem.subsubitem', each item has to be a package, but the last one; the last item could be a module or package, but this cannot be a class or function or variable identified in the previous item.

CONCLUSION

Research across almost all fields has become more data-oriented, impacting both the job opportunities and the required skills. While more data and methods of evaluating them are becoming obtainable, more data-dependent aspects of the economy, society, and daily life are becoming. Whenever it comes to data science, Python is a tool necessary with all sorts of advantages. It is flexible and continually improving because it is open-source. Python already has a number of valuable libraries, and it cannot be ignored that it can be combined with other languages (like Java) and current frameworks. Long story short - Python is an amazing method for data science.

www.ingramcontent.com/pod-product-compliance
Lightning Source LLC
LaVergne TN
LVHW051222050326
832903LV00028B/2207